Case Studies on Diversity and Social Justice Education

Case Studies on Diversity and Social Justice Education offers pre- and in-service educators an opportunity to analyze and reflect upon a variety of realistic case studies related to educational equity and social justice. Each case, written in an engaging narrative style, presents a complex but common classroom scenario in which an inequity or injustice is in play. These cases allow educators to practice the process of considering a range of contextual factors, checking their own biases, and making immediate and longer-term decisions about how to create and sustain equitable learning environments for all students.

The book begins with a seven-point process for examining case studies. Largely lacking from existing case study collections, this framework guides readers through the process of identifying, examining, reflecting on, and taking concrete steps to resolve challenges related to diversity and equity in schools. The cases themselves present everyday examples of the ways in which racism, sexism, homophobia and heterosexism, class inequities, language bias, religious oppression, and other equity and diversity concerns affect students, teachers, families, and other members of our school communities. They involve classroom issues that are relevant to all grade levels and all content areas, allowing significant flexibility in how and with whom they are used. Although organized topically, the intersection of these issues is stressed throughout the cases, reflecting the multifaceted way in which they play out in real life. All cases conclude with a series of questions to guide discussion and a section of facilitator notes, called Points for Consideration. This unique feature provides valuable insight for understanding the complexities of each case.

Paul C. Gorski is an Associate Professor of Integrative Studies, teaching in the Social Justice and Education concentrations at George Mason University, and the founder of EdChange.

Seema G. Pothini is a former classroom teacher, cultural integration specialist, and teacher trainer who now serves as an equity and diversity consultant.

Case Studies on Diversity and Social Justice Education

Paul C. Gorski and Seema G. Pothini

Routledge
Taylor & Francis Group

NEW YORK AND LONDON

First published 2014
by Routledge
711 Third Avenue, New York, NY 10017

and by Routledge
2 Park Square, Milton Park, Abingdon, Oxon OX14 4RN

Routledge is an imprint of the Taylor & Francis Group, an informa business

© 2014 Taylor & Francis

Library of Congress Cataloging in Publication Data
Gorski, Paul C.
  Case studies on diversity and social justice education / by Paul C. Gorski and Seema G. Pothini.
    pages cm
  Includes bibliographical references and index.
  1. Multicultural education—Case studies.   2. Social justice—Study and teaching.   I. Pothini, Seema G.   II. Title.
  LC1099.G67 2013
  370.117—dc23

                                                                2013018125

ISBN: 978–0–415–65824–9 (hbk)
ISBN: 978–0–415–65825–6 (pbk)
ISBN: 978–0–203–07620–0 (ebk)

Typeset in Adobe Caslon
by RefineCatch Limited, Bungay, Suffolk, UK

Printed and bound in the United States of America by Publishers Graphics, LLC on sustainably sourced paper.

Dedication

Paul: For Mr. Hill, a champion of educational equity and my middle school chorus teacher. Nobody did more to inspire me to become an educator (despite the fact that I still can't sing).

Seema: For my parents, whose strength and experiences have taught me that no obstacle is too large. For my children and husband for being incredibly loving, supportive, and helpful in all my endeavors. And for the students I have been blessed to work with as an educator; your stories continue to fuel my passion to ensure equity in our schools.

Contents

Directory of Cases by Topic   ix

Foreword   xiii

1   Introduction   **1**

     The Case Method   6

     The Rest of This Book   8

2   Analyzing Cases Using the Equity Literacy Framework   **11**

     Equity Literacy Framework   11

     Case Analysis: An Equity Literacy Process   13

     A Few Final Thoughts   20

3   Cases on Socioeconomic Status   **21**

     Case 3.1: Chocolate Bar Fundraiser   21

     Case 3.2: A Class Lesson in Etiquette   24

     Case 3.3: Student Protest   26

     Case 3.4: High Expectations or Unrealistic Goals?   29

4   Cases on Religion   **33**

     Case 4.1: The Winter Party   33

     Case 4.2: Christmas Lights?   36

     Case 4.3: A Difference in Perspectives   38

     Case 4.4: Islamophobic Read-Aloud   40

5   Cases on Ethnicity and Culture   **45**

     Case 5.1: Generalizations on Display   45

     Case 5.2: Not Time for Stories   47

Case 5.3: Inappropriate Language   50
Case 5.4: Multicultural Day Parade   52
Case 5.5: A Place to Study   54

6   **Cases on Race**   **57**
Case 6.1: Task Force   57
Case 6.2: Teaching Race with *Huckleberry Finn*   60
Case 6.3: Diverse Friends Day   62
Case 6.4: Terms of Endearment   64
Case 6.5: An Uncomfortable Field Trip   67

7   **Cases on Sex, Gender, and Gender Identity**   **71**
Case 7.1: Boys versus Girls Trivia Contest   71
Case 7.2: Gender Bias with a Smile   73
Case 7.3: Timmy's Gender Nonconformity   76
Case 7.4: Internet Objectification   78

8   **Cases on (Dis)Ability**   **83**
Case 8.1: A "Surprise" Fire Drill   83
Case 8.2: Insufficient Accommodations   85
Case 8.3: Nut Allergy   87

9   **Cases on Sexual Orientation**   **91**
Case 9.1: A New Club   91
Case 9.2: Date Auction   93
Case 9.3: Outed at School   95
Case 9.4: Two Moms   98

10   **Cases on Language**   **103**
Case 10.1: Student Translator   103
Case 10.2: English Only   105
Case 10.3: Family Night   107

11   **Cases on Immigrant Status**   **111**
Case 11.1: An Assigned Nickname   111
Case 11.2: I'm not Black   113
Case 11.3: A Legacy of Privilege on the Soccer Field   115
Case 11.4: Parent Involvement   118
Case 11.5: My Uncle   121

**Appendix A: The Equity Literacy Case Analysis
          Worksheet**   **125**

Appendix B: Points for Consideration   **127**

References   159

Directory of Cases by Topic

Curriculum

Case 3.2: A Class Lesson in Etiquette
Case 4.4: Islamophobic Read-Aloud
Case 5.1: Generalizations on Display
Case 6.2: Teaching Race with *Huckleberry Finn*
Case 7.2: Gender Bias with a Smile

Pedagogy and Instruction

Case 4.3: A Difference in Perspectives
Case 5.2: Not Time for Stories
Case 6.5: An Uncomfortable Field Trip
Case 7.1: Boys versus Girls Trivia Contest
Case 8.2: Insufficient Accommodations
Case 9.4: Two Moms

Discipline, Engagement, and Classroom "Management"

Case 3.3: Student Protest
Case 4.2: Christmas Lights?

Case 5.2: Not Time for Stories
Case 10.1: Student Translator

School and Classroom Policy and Practice

Case 3.1: Chocolate Bar Fundraiser
Case 8.1: A "Surprise" Fire Drill
Case 8.3: Nut Allergy
Case 9.1: A New Club
Case 10.2: English Only
Case 11.2: I'm not Black
Case 11.3: A Legacy of Privilege on the Soccer Field

School Culture

Case 3.3: Student Protest
Case 3.4: High Expectations or Unrealistic Goals?
Case 4.1: The Winter Party
Case 4.3: A Difference in Perspectives
Case 5.1: Generalizations on Display
Case 9.3: Outed at School
Case 11.5: My Uncle

Programs

Case 3.4: High Expectations or Unrealistic Goals?
Case 5.4: Multicultural Day Parade
Case 6.3: Diverse Friends Day
Case 9.2: Date Auction
Case 10.3: Family Night

Parent and Community Involvement and Relations

Case 4.1: The Winter Party
Case 5.5: A Place to Study
Case 6.1: Task Force
Case 10.1: Student Translator

Case 10.3: Family Night
Case 11.1: An Assigned Nickname
Case 11.4: Parent Involvement
Case 11.5: My Uncle

Bias and Bullying

Case 3.4: High Expectations or Unrealistic Goals?
Case 4.2: Christmas Lights?
Case 5.3: Inappropriate Language
Case 6.4: Terms of Endearment
Case 7.2: Gender Bias with a Smile
Case 7.3: Timmy's Gender Nonconformity
Case 7.4: Internet Objectification

Foreword

So often when we wrestle with topics in college courses or in training for a profession, the instruction is in the abstract. The situation in which the doctor, or the teacher, or the lawyer finds her-or himself is described one or two steps removed from reality. In my case, my education classes, while interesting, seemed totally disconnected from what went on with the youth I student-taught each day. If the young people I taught were presented at all, they were described as "data," or part of "trends," or the result of "demographics." When I began teaching on my own I was starting from scratch, learning the rituals and rhythms of the school day without a hint of preparation from the texts I had read, the theoretical constructs I had studied. I learned that the early morning hour, before the first bell, was the best time to spend with students who arrived at 7 a.m., who grabbed their breakfast across the street at McDonalds, and who needed a place to sit and eat. I learned that the young girl in the back of the class who had no warm footwear in the winter was not neglected by her parents, but rather was homeless and had lost her pair of too-small boots as she shifted from one place to another in order to sleep.

I began to understand that the stories my students had to tell were in no way stories for which I was prepared. Each young woman or man who sat in my third-floor classroom was a mix of poverty or wealth, culture, religion, personality, and inquisitiveness. It took living with them each day to grasp their variety, their complexity. Very rarely did I hear about youth like Sothol in classes I took in college: a boy from Cambodia, raised by his big sister. And even when I did talk with other teachers about a child's progress, his class, race, religion, and culture were often treated with short shrift.

I know that many universities, colleges, and professional development initiatives are making an effort to change their programs from being theoretical and abstract to being more responsive to the issues that students and teachers face every day. I am often a speaker in education classes and staff trainings and I am heartened by the progress. Yet I also have met many teachers who have little awareness of white privilege or economic advantage. They drop phrases like "It's too bad, our students could learn if they had a father in the home, books in their room, a computer in their house, or even a better apartment in a safer part of the city."

What this book does is give readers the chance to think about schools and their amazing collection of children in ways that you might not have thought about before. This collection of cases can expand your mind, forcing you to take in the sociopolitical context of schooling in realistic, applied ways. It is written in straightforward, non-jargon language. It presents dilemmas, situations, and cases that come from the dusty corridors, the ramshackle teacher lounges, the noisy, vibrant, and sometimes difficult classrooms that are the roots of public education. I would have appreciated having this book before I stood in front of my class of seventh graders that first September morning so many years ago because it challenges its readers to open their minds to the story behind the story: the system of poverty, or racism, or language barriers, or other elements of society that can influence all that happens in our students' lives. We are not provided with one right answer or one correct response; rather, we are asked to contemplate many variables that are part of each scenario. We are asked to develop what Gloria Ladson-Billings describes as a "state of being" when we think about student and parent reactions to our school's demands. This state requires us to think in terms of short-term solutions to a situation, as well as to address longer-term policy decisions in our buildings.

Case Studies on Diversity and Social Justice Education presents many scenarios that challenge us to think beyond what we see, what we "know" at the moment. It asks us to grapple with real and complex issues depicted in school settings. What a gift to have the chance to practice an inclusive way of thinking about schooling so that when we do arrive in a classroom, when we do push those desks into small group formations and turn on the music player in the pre-dawn hour before the buses roll up, we can be ready. We can be open to thinking in terms of solutions instead of judgments.

I believe that it is only through working with realities, with stories, and information, and the words of children and youth themselves, that we begin to understand all that needs to be done to provide economic and racial equity in our schools. This is the place to start. Expanding our observation to include all aspects of the whole child is essential for understanding the girl in the first row who squints at the board or the child who has a headache, sitting with his hand over his swollen jaw. Knowing how to make sure these children get the resources they need to become leaders, doctors, construction workers, or even teachers is vital to making decisions about how we run our schools, our districts, our cities, and our country.

This book also gives teachers and principals, counselors and social workers, teaching assistants and lunchroom workers the possibility of activism. It asks us to open our minds and gives us practice doing just that. Education activism can begin in our schoolyards over a play-ground that lacks equipment and can spread to our city councils and zoning bodies, our mayors' offices and our legislatures. We have a chance to be instrumental in bringing about true equity beyond anything we could have imagined while sitting in teacher preparation classes full of abstraction and jargon. In each story in this book and in the multi-perspective responses and questions presented here, we learn to think in ways that expand our minds outward. Examining these cases can prepare us to find both short- and long-term solutions to complex problems—solutions we previously might never have envisioned. To think in a broader context, to release ourselves from instant judgments, to look at a child from a prism of possibilities, is no small thing. This book gives us this—this state of being.

Julie Landsman
Author, *A White Teacher Talks About Race*

1

INTRODUCTION

Samantha, a vivacious seventh grader at Hillside School, a middle school in the predominantly low-income mountainous outskirts of northern Virginia, loves science class. "Are we doing lab work today?" she often asks Ms. Grady, her science teacher, as she hurries into the classroom. By all apparent accounts, Samantha has a gift for the sciences, too. She aces all of her quizzes and tests and regularly helps classmates who are struggling with experiments.

This makes it particularly difficult for Ms. Grady to understand why Samantha rarely turns in her science homework. Wondering whether there was an issue at home, Ms. Grady has touched base several times with her colleagues who have Samantha's younger siblings in their classes to see whether they were noticing similar patterns. To the contrary, she learned that her younger siblings always turn in their homework.

Ms. Grady also has reached out to Samantha every way she knows how, from pleading with her—"You could have an A in this class if you only did your homework!"—to offering to give her more advanced work that might engage her in new ways. On several occasions she has asked Samantha why she rarely turns in her homework. "Don't you understand how important this is?" she asks. "Please tell me what's going on so I can help you be successful in my class."

"It's nothing," Samantha typically responds. "I'll do it next time. I promise."

Ms. Grady has attempted to reach out to Samantha's parents, too. She has called their home several times, hoping to speak with them about the importance of homework, both for honing Samantha's science skills and for helping to secure her future spot in more advanced high school science classes. Unfortunately, these efforts have only caused Ms. Grady more frustration. Regardless of how often she calls Samantha's parents, nobody answers. To make matters worse, the family does not have voicemail or an answering machine. *Imagine how successful Samantha could be if only her parents cared enough to support her education*, Ms. Grady has often thought to herself.

As a conscientious teacher, Ms. Grady wants to support Samantha. She wants to continue encouraging her. On the other hand, she has roomfuls of other students who also need her attention. And, when it comes down to it, Ms. Grady's grading policy is clear: students are allowed to turn in one homework assignment one day late without penalty—she calls this her "life happens" rule; but in every other instance, failure to turn in homework results in a grade of "0" for that assignment. If she decides to bend her policy for Samantha, she risks being unfair to other students, some of whom struggle on quizzes, tests, or class participation, but always do their homework.

Nothing is simple when it comes to educational equity. We all can agree that every student *ought to* have access to equitable educational opportunity—that a student's (or, for that matter, a teacher's or administrator's) racial identity, socioeconomic status, sexual orientation, gender identity, or home language should not determine her level of access to educational and vocational opportunity or predict her grades or her likelihood of graduating from high school. But do we agree on how to find our way to an equitable educational system? Do we agree, for that matter, on how to create an equitable school or classroom?

We believe that one perpetual struggle that impedes us, as educators, in our quest to create more equitable and just schools is a tendency to try to solve complex problems or address complex conditions with simple, immediate solutions. Consider, for example, the time and resources that schools across the U.S. have invested in attempting to redress achievement gaps by training their teachers on culture- or identity-specific "learning styles"; on the "girl brain" and "boy brain"; on the "culture of poverty." We, too, understand the lure of these approaches. We share the sense of urgency that accompanies our own roomfuls of students who cannot, and should not have to, wait for the educational revolution to come along before their learning needs are addressed more effectively. These approaches are easy to learn and easier to implement. *Here are the ten things every teacher should know about Latino boys.* We can incorporate them into our teaching tomorrow.

However, although they might be convenient for the teacher, they have not been shown to bolster student engagement. They are simple and straightforward and, unfortunately, more a *reflection of* inequity than a *challenge to* inequity.

For example, research has shown that teaching to particular learning styles is ineffective because students' learning styles and learning needs fluctuate depending on what they are learning, the context in which they're learning, and their confidence with the material, among other factors. Moreover, identity-specific learning styles simply do not exist. The diversity of preferred learning modalities *within* individual identity groups—African American boys, for example—is just as great as the diversity of preferred learning modalities *between* identity groups.

Complicating matters is the fact that a considerable portion of disparities in educational outcomes such as academic performance and graduation rates are symptoms of conditions that fall outside our individual spheres of influence. For example, we cannot control families' access to living wage work or healthcare. Of course, we can and, we would argue, we *should* at the very least be aware of these conditions and how they affect our students' lives and experiences because they also affect our students' interactions with us and with the schools in which we work.

So, upon reading Samantha's story, it might be easy to draw on popular explanations for her consistent inattention to homework or for her parents' or guardians' lack of responsiveness to Ms. Grady's calls. *If they cared about her education,* you might reason, *they would make themselves available to her teacher and they certainly would insist that she do her homework.* If only it were that simple.

One day after school Ms. Grady approaches Mr. Burns, a social studies teacher at Hillside who had taken a particular interest in Samantha during the previous academic year. Mr. Burns nods as Ms. Grady shares her concerns: Samantha regularly aces quizzes and tests, but rarely completes her homework. "I've tried to reach her parents," she explains with exasperation, "but they never respond."

"I know," Mr. Burns says. "Brilliant young woman. I had the same experience with her. I didn't know what to think until I decided to pay her family a visit at home." Having grown up in the area and attended Hillside as a low-income student, Mr. Burns bristled at some of his colleagues' deficit-laden perceptions of the local community. Contrasting their presumptions of the "laziness" of poor people, his own parents had worked two or three jobs at a time during his childhood, usually at minimum wage, just to get by. Now, as a teacher at Hillside, he regularly visits families in their homes, marveling at their resilience in the face of the scarcity of healthcare services, living wage work, and the types of basic infrastructure that less rural communities just a dozen miles away take for granted.

It never had occurred to Ms. Grady to visit Samantha's home, much less to show up unannounced. "Wow!" she responds, taken aback by her colleague's "direct action" approach to student success. "What did you learn?"

"A *lot*," he answers, explaining that Samantha's father finally found a steady job four months after the local mill shut down, but that it requires him to commute 90 minutes to and from the city each day. He took the mid-day shift, noon to 8:30 p.m., so he could see the kids to school each morning. As she has done for years, Samantha's mother continues to piece together multiple jobs, beginning her work day at 5 a.m. on a restaurant cleaning crew, then doing a six-hour shift at a retail store before heading to the local middle school as part of the nighttime cleaning crew. "She usually sneaks in the door around 11 p.m., an hour or so after her husband, trying not to wake the kids," Mr. Burns explains.

"So that's why they're not around to answer my calls in the evenings," Ms. Grady replies softly, as if to herself.

"Right. But that's also why Samantha struggles to do her homework. From the moment she gets home from school until her dad returns from work, she's babysitting Francis and Kevin, her younger siblings. She's busy taking them to the playground, cooking them dinner, helping them with *their* homework."

"Well," Ms. Grady reflects, "that explains why her siblings' home-work is always in on time and how well Samantha does helping her classmates with their work."

"A lot of practice," Mr. Burns says, nodding.

"Now all I have to do is figure out what to do about Samantha's grade. And I wonder how many of my other students are in similar situations," Ms. Grady says.

"If you come up with the perfect solution," Mr. Burns offers with a chuckle, "please let me know."

There are, of course, no perfect answers or solutions when it comes to the complexities of diversity and social justice. There exists no magic formula for solving the conundrum in which Ms. Grady finds herself. This is why, in our estimation, we must develop and hone the sorts of competencies that help us to make sense out of real-life messiness. Otherwise, we risk allowing ourselves to be swayed by popular mythology ("poor people do not care enough about their children's education") and how we've been socialized to buy into that mythology when we are responding to these sorts of situations. We risk responding without a contoured understanding for why certain conditions exist in our classrooms and schools.

So, what would you do if you were Ms. Grady? What would you do in the immediate term? Would you adjust your policies to accommo-date Samantha, a gifted student whose grade is suffering for reasons beyond her control? Would doing so threaten your commitment to expressing high expectations for all of your students? Would you look for new ways to reach out to her family?

Just as importantly, how would you respond in the longer term, knowing that other students might be in similar situations? How, if at all, might you adjust the way in which you give homework or how you weigh it when you are calculating grades? How would you use what you've learned to become a more equitable educator, not just for your current students but for your future students?

Certainly, in our role as teachers, as much as we might want to do so, we cannot control some of the bigger life situations in which our students and their families find themselves. We might not have the power, as individuals, to see to it that profitable corporations do not move their mill operations in search of more profit; we probably don't have the power to force employers to pay their employees a living wage so that all parents and guardians will have more time at home with their children. We *do*, however, have the power to understand how our students' lives outside school—the repressions they and their families face, the inequities with which the contend, the resilience they demonstrate in overcoming whatever challenges are in their way—inform the way in which they experience us, as teachers, and school. We have the power to strengthen our abilities to create equitable learning environments and to maintain high expectations for all students by considering these contextual factors in addition to the everyday practicalities of our work as we shape our professional practice.

The Case Method

One tool—and, in our experience, a particularly effective one—for strengthening those abilities is what is commonly called the "case method." The premise of the case method is that by analyzing real-life scenarios based on actual events, such as the situation involving Samantha and Ms. Grady, we can practice applying theoretical ideas (such as *educational equity*) to on-the-ground professional practice (Darling-Hammond, 2006). The case method allows us to practice stepping through a process of considering a range of perspectives and angles; to practice seeing the full complexity of everyday classroom situations; and, as a result, to reflect on the perspectives, angles, and complexities we might not see in the chaos of our day-to-day work lives. In this sense, the case method is, in the words of William and Margaret Naumes (1999, p11), an "active pedagogical practice," an applicative process designed to build our capacities for evaluating and implementing mindful responses to complex, and often inequitable, school and classroom conditions (Leonard & Cook, 2010). In fact, studies have demonstrated the case method's effectiveness in deepening critical thinking abilities, problem-solving skills, and other competencies in professionals from a variety of fields, including social work (Jones, 2005), medicine (Tarnvik, 2007), forensic science (Noblitt et al, 2010), public policy (Foster et al, 2010), and, of course, education (Brown & Kraehe, 2010; Heitzmann, 2008).

Richard Foster and his colleagues (2010, p523) explain, in this spirit, the nature of a case method "case":

> The teaching case is a story, a narrative if you will, usually based on actual events and told with a definite teaching purpose. It does not have a correct answer or obvious solution, relying instead on the nature of the real world where answers are difficult to come by and solutions are always contested. [We] are introduced to the need to think carefully, to listen to the points made by others and to evaluate those arguments, to review alternative courses of action and their efficacy, and to interpret real-world experience.

This, we think, is among the most formidable challenges that the case method poses to current and future teachers. In this era of high-stakes testing and standardization, when many of us are feeling increasingly desperate for practical solutions to complex problems, the idea that there might not be, that there usually *isn't*, a practical solution or "right answer" can be daunting. The point of examining a case, as we see it, is not to be constrained by boxes—*this* is correct, so *this* must be incorrect—but rather to muddle through the gray areas by considering all that makes them gray. The case method allows us to do this in a way that few other pedagogical methods allow.

This muddling is especially important when it comes to matters of equity and diversity. After all, none of us wants to contribute to racial, or class, or gender inequities in our classrooms. Each of us wants Samantha and all of her classmates to succeed. The trouble is, we might not always understand how, even if unintentionally, we might be helping to create some of the barriers to their learning, despite our beliefs about educational equity.

The other important diversity and social justice benefit of the case method is that it challenges us to question our own mental models by examining classroom situations through a variety of lenses (Gallucci, 2006). It challenges us to practice asking the questions we previously might never have thought to ask; to reconsider old ways of thinking in light of new understandings. How do we see Samantha's situation differently when we reject the old stereotype about poor people who don't value education? How do we relate differently to her parents when we see their unavailability in the evening as a marker of their *commitment* to providing for their children rather than their *lack of commitment* to their children's schooling? How might we think differently about ourselves as equitable educators when we learn better how to see past our prejudices and consider a broader picture? These are the sorts of questions that cannot be answered by theory alone or by memorizing "five practical strategies for teaching all low-income students." They require deeper, more critical, reflection: the kind encouraged by the case method.

With this in mind, we chose to write *Case Studies on Diversity and Social Justice Education* for several reasons. First, we have observed how the case method has aided our own work preparing teachers and ourselves to think and teach more equitably and justly. We, as educators, have experienced situations similar to those described in our cases but have found too few opportunities to process what has happened as mindfully as possible. These cases provide an opportunity to practice doing just that. Additionally, as we mentioned earlier, it can be particularly challenging, without practice, for us to "see" what is happening in our classrooms without being constrained by our existing biases, ideologies, and mental models. The case method provides opportunities for us to strengthen these competencies by practicing thoughtful analysis and problem-solving skills. We have constructed the cases purposefully to challenge ourselves and our readers to consider our teaching in light of what Nieto and Bode (2011) call the *sociopolitical context of schooling*. Taking account of this sociopolitical context requires us to recognize the relationship between the kinds of inequities that plague our schools and larger societal inequities, even when we don't see those larger conditions as part of our purview.

It is our intention, and indeed our hope, that our book will create this kind of deeper reflection about equity, diversity, and social justice concerns in schools and, by doing so, encourage readers to consider how they might ensure that *all* students have the opportunity to excel—that all students will have equitable access to the best possible education we can provide.

The Rest of This Book

Without question, the essence of this book is in the cases themselves: about three dozen scenarios based on, or approximating, actual school and classroom events we have witnessed or heard about. Each case, written in a narrative, literary style, presents a complex, yet fairly common, school or classroom scenario in which an inequity or injustice—sometimes implicit, sometimes explicit—might be in play. It is up to you, the reader, to weigh the situation and decide how to respond. Issues include racism and white privilege, sexism and male privilege, heterosexism and heteronormativity, poverty and economic injustice, language bias and linguicism, religious-based oppression, and various intersections of these and other conditions.

In order to encourage the sort of complex analysis we believe best prepares us to understand and justly respond to inequitable classroom and school conditions, we follow this introduction, in Chapter 2, by outlining a case analysis process constructed and honed through our combined decades' worth of teaching and teacher professional development experience. We also step back through the case incorporated into this introduction in order to demonstrate how to apply the case analysis process.

Chapters 3 through 11 contain cases specific to particular identities and oppressions. Each case in these chapters includes a section of facilitator notes—we call them "Points for Consideration"—that include recommendations for the sorts of issues and concepts that should be highlighted. Each case also includes a series of questions intended to encourage deep, complex, reflection on these issues and concepts. We would like to point out that the division of the cases into these chapters is imprecise in the sense that some of the cases address multiple identities and oppressions. Finally, although we specify in each case whether it occurred in an elementary school, middle school, or high school, almost all of the cases can be easily adapted for any school context.

Although most of the cases in this book are based on real scenarios we have witnessed or heard about, we were careful to change the names of people, schools, and places in order to mask the identities of those involved.

2
ANALYZING CASES USING THE EQUITY LITERACY FRAMEWORK

There are countless approaches to analyzing case studies. Believe us, we know. We examined dozens of them in preparation for writing this book. Many were very discipline specific, focused, for example, on corporate law cases, or electrical engineering challenges, or disability rights in the workplace. None felt quite right for a book of cases designed to help educators strengthen their understandings of the ways—even the little, subtle ways—in which bias and inequity play out in school settings or practice, responding to that bias and inequity in constructive, effective ways. So we turned to a framework that, at its core, is designed for just that purpose.

Equity Literacy Framework

Our goal, in the end, was to write cases and pose questions that would boost in teachers, counselors, teacher aides, administrators, and others what our colleague, Katy Swalwell (2011) has called *equity literacy*. We are equity literate, Katy has explained, when we are "knowledgeable about the inequity that exists in our midst" (Swalwell, 2011, p. 13). Part of what sets equity literacy apart from cultural competence, intercultural relations, and many of the other popular frameworks for thinking about equity and diversity in school is that it encourages us to understand dynamics related to, say, race or gender identity, not just in terms of interpersonal or cultural conflict, but also as part of bigger, broader social and cultural conditions.

Thinking back to Samantha, cultural competence asks us to consider how we might understand her culture better so that we can communicate with her or her family more effectively. Obviously, this is a noble and important step, so long as we realize that culture is an individual attribute and not a whole set of values and dispositions that we can attribute freely to any person who happens to be from a low-income family. The problem, though, is that if we constrain our understandings of Samantha and her homework situation to culture, we miss all other sorts of important dynamics that are less about Samantha's culture than about the challenges she faces as a child in a low-income family. If we fail to see that bigger picture, we limit the likelihood that we will craft strategies for overcoming these challenges that are holistic, just, and effective.

For example, if we focus solely on Samantha's culture, we might spend our energy seeking different ways to communicate to her and her family how important it is for her to do her homework. The problem is, their attitudes about the importance of her homework really are not the problem. There's something deeper, more complex, going on that has to do with opportunity, access, social conditions, and the messiness of socioeconomic status and class inequity, and we worry that cultural competence will not help us see that something.

This is why we decided to create a new process, based on the principles of equity literacy, for examining equity-related education cases and crafting responses to the problems they pose. The equity literacy framework is built, in essence, to move us into the messiness. It forces us to consider, simultaneously, things as micro-level as our individual biases and as macro-level as societal inequities. It challenges us to reflect upon how our instructional decisions affect students and how life experiences outside the classroom affect them. As a result it better positions us to respond to classroom challenges involving the complexities of diversity and social justice in suitably complex and equitable ways.

The equity literacy framework is comprised of "the skills and dispositions that enable us to recognize, respond to, and redress conditions that deny some students access to the educational opportunities enjoyed by their peers" and "the skills and dispositions that allow us to create and sustain equitable learning environments for all families and students" (Gorski, in press). The four foundational skills of equity

Table 2.1 The Four Skills of Equity Literacy

EQUITY LITERACY ABILITIES	EXAMPLES OF ASSOCIATED SKILLS AND DISPOSITIONS
Ability to *recognize* biases and inequities, including those that are subtle	Equity literate educators: • notice even subtle bias in classroom materials, classroom interactions, and school policies; and • reject deficit views that locate the sources of outcome inequalities (such as test score disparities) as existing within students' "cultures" rather than as resulting from inequitable educational opportunity.
Ability to *respond to* biases and inequities in the immediate term	Equity literate educators: • have the facilitation skills and content knowledge necessary to intervene effectively when biases or inequities, such as gender bias or sexism, arise in the classroom; and • foster conversations with colleagues about bias and equity concerns at their schools.
Ability to *redress* biases and inequities in the long term	Equity literate educators: • advocate against inequitable school practices, such as racially or economically biased tracking, and advocate for equitable school practices; and • never confuse *celebrating diversity* with *equity*, such as by responding to racial conflict with cultural celebrations.
Ability to *create and sustain* a bias-free and equitable learning environment	Equity literate educators: • express high expectations for all students through higher-order pedagogies and curricula; and • cultivate a classroom environment in which students feel free to express themselves openly and honestly.

Source: adapted from Gorski (in press)

literacy are summarized in Table 2.1. These, we realized, were the very skills we hoped our cases would foster in educators.

Case Analysis: An Equity Literacy Process

Our process for analyzing educational cases, assembled to strengthen in educators the four foundational skills of equity literacy, is comprised of seven steps, summarized in Figure 2.1. The steps are accumulative,

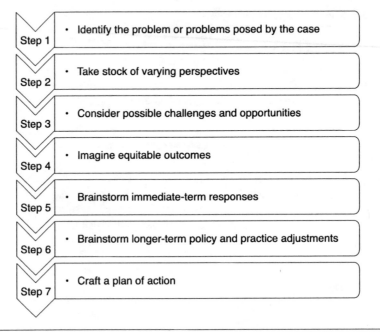

Figure 2.1 Seven steps in the equity literacy case analysis approach.

building steadily and holistically toward a set of informed, mindful responses to often complex classroom and school situations. They ask us to peel away layers of the proverbial onion, never settling for quick, simple responses that rely too heavily on our predispositions.

In what follows we describe each of the seven steps of the equity literacy process for analyzing educational cases. In order to demonstrate the process in action, we also apply the steps to the scenario regarding Samantha and her science homework explored in Chapter 1. (An abbreviated, printable version of the process can be found in Appendix A.)

As you will see, we did not design the case analysis process to guide you toward a *correct* response. Hand this process and any case from this book to ten teachers or school administrators and chances are they will come up with ten different plans of action. Instead, we designed it to help you practice using your own unique insights, your own knowledge about students and their families, and your own expertise with school and classroom dynamics in order to respond, as effectively and equitably as possible, to the types of biases and inequities that inevitably crop up in schools. It is more an art than a science; more a willingness to dig, and dig, and dig deeply than an ability to calculate quickly.

This also is why, humbled by our own limitations, we encourage you, whenever possible, to analyze the cases in this book in groups. Almost as important as reflecting upon our unique individual analyses of each case is reflecting upon why people with different combinations of identities and life experiences might interpret the cases so differently.

Step 1: Identify the Problem or Problems Posed by the Case

Many of the biases and inequities students face in school are implicit and unintentional, hidden in day-to-day practices, school traditions, and quiet interactions. It can be especially difficult for us, as educators, not to immediately recognize the sorts of challenges that students or families face when we never have faced those challenges ourselves. If you have never been tasked with caring for younger siblings after school, for instance, it might be easy never to imagine that this is a responsibility many low-income students, such as Samantha, have. This is why we urge you, during Step 1, to read between the lines a bit. Practice seeing the conditions and contexts you might not usually see.

Begin by naming the challenges or problems (or potential problems) that are explicit and immediately apparent to you. It's obvious, for example, that Ms. Grady is concerned about Samantha not doing her homework and how this is affecting Samantha's grade. It is clear, as well, that having tried and failed to reach Samantha's parents, Ms. Grady is running out of strategies. Once she learns more about Samantha's situation, Ms. Grady finds herself in somewhat of a bind. How, if at all, should she modify her homework policy? These, in essence, are the concerns at the surface of the story.

Once you have a grasp of those more obvious dynamics, try to dig a little deeper. Read between the lines. Look for less explicit, not-so-obvious examples of existing or potential bias, inequity, interpersonal tensions, stereotypes, prejudices, or assumptions. What does the case tell us about school or classroom policy, about instructional practices or curricula, about individuals' attitudes that might hint at something deeper than those surface-level biases and inequities? Consider, for example, Ms. Grady's assumption that Samantha's parents don't care about her education. At first glance this dynamic might seem unimportant. Overall Ms. Grady appears to care sincerely about Samantha and, upon speaking with Mr. Burns, she seems open enough to the possibility of rethinking her assumptions. However, we also know that Samantha was hesitant to tell Ms. Grady the truth about why she wasn't doing her homework. Is it possible that she sensed in Ms. Grady the biases evident in her initial assumptions?

Remember, there are no right or wrong answers here—no single "problem" that everybody should identify in a case. Different people will identify different problems, and that's just fine. In fact, it's an opportunity for us to learn from each other what we tend to see and what we might tend to miss.

Step 2: Take Stock of Varying Perspectives

Our case has at least a couple of obvious stakeholders. Most obvious, perhaps, are Samantha and Ms. Grady. In the most immediate term, we might think, Ms. Grady's decision about her homework policy will affect Samantha, her science grade, and her ability to land a spot in advanced science courses later in her school career. Our first task, then, for Step 2 is, as best we can, to walk in Ms. Grady's and Samantha's shoes. How might they, given who they are in relation to one another, be experiencing the situation?

Ms. Grady, we might suggest, is a caring and frustrated teacher who wants Samantha to succeed. Perhaps you can imagine her, with all of her good intentions, being frustrated, maybe even confused, with her inability to reach Samantha's parents. Samantha, on the other hand, as a low-income student, might be used to teachers who, despite their good intentions, make assumptions about her and her family. Clearly she enjoys science, so chances are she *wants* to do the homework Ms. Grady assigns. She is not dodging the responsibility. If Ms. Grady wants to find an equitable solution to the situation, she probably needs to be careful not to treat Samantha as though she's purposefully breaking the rules.

Complicating matters, despite being at the center of the scenario, Samantha and Ms. Grady are only two of many affected parties. Samantha's parents, whose other two children, Frances and Kevin, also attend the school and in the future might even have Ms. Grady as a teacher, are involved. Ms. Grady's decision on how to resolve the issue at hand will have an impact upon the whole family. Then there are Samantha's classmates, the "bystanders." How might Ms. Grady's decisions affect other students who are from families in poverty? How might it look to any of Samantha's classmates if Ms. Grady makes an exception for her? We might consider, as well, Mr. Burns and his view as somebody who grew up in a situation similar to Samantha's and feels the weight of some of his colleagues' biases. We might also consider other teachers and a broad array of other possible constituents.

We do encourage you to try to find some balance between focusing only on the most obvious stakeholders and broadening your focus so much that the analysis becomes unwieldy. Start with the immediate participants and then, at the very least, the ring of constituents around them.

Step 3: Consider Possible Challenges and Opportunities

Given the varied perspectives explored in Step 2, our next task is to imagine the potential challenges and opportunities presented by the case. Start with the individuals involved. We might surmise that Ms. Grady has an opportunity to develop a deeper understanding of low-income students—of both the hurdles they might face and the resiliencies they demonstrate. Other opportunities abound. She can craft a more equitable homework policy, connect with Samantha in new ways, or even initiate a conversation about class bias with her colleagues. Of course, she also faces a number of challenges, not least of which is overcoming her own biases. Another challenge, you might observe, is her inability to reach Samantha's parents using the strategies she's accustomed to using, making it more difficult to elicit their problem-solving collaboration. What sorts of opportunities and challenges does the case present for Samantha? For her classmates?

We also want to consider the *institutional* challenges and opportunities. For instance, based on what we learned from Mr. Burns, we might assume, by way of challenges, that Ms. Grady might not get a tremendous amount of support if she chose to enact a homework policy that did not conform to those of her colleagues. An institutional opportunity, on the other hand, might be the chance to collaborate toward more equitable school-wide policies and practices in order to more effectively engage low-income students and families.

Again, remember to use your analysis from Steps 1 and 2 to inform your consideration of possible challenges and opportunities. One goal in later steps will be to develop responses to cases that take optimal advantage of the opportunities while navigating the challenges effectively.

Step 4: Imagine Equitable Outcomes

Building on the contextual understandings that you have gained by taking stock of stakeholders' perspectives and considering possible challenges and opportunities, we turn, in Step 4, to imagining what a fair and equitable resolution to the situation might look like. This is a critical step, as Steps 5 through 7 are designed to facilitate the process of working toward the outcomes we define in Step 4.

A few guiding principles can be especially helpful as we imagine what we hope to achieve by seeking resolutions to the cases in this book. First, it's important to distinguish *equitable* outcomes from *equal* outcomes. Equality, as we see it, connotes *sameness*. Equity, on the other hand, connotes *fairness*. Equity takes context into account. The equality-minded educator, for instance, might think it's unfair for schools to spend more resources or adjust policies or practices for students whose families are in poverty. The equity-minded educator, on the other hand, might recognize all the ways in which people in poverty are denied all manner of opportunities that their wealthier peers take for granted and think it's only fair for schools to play a mitigating role. In Samantha's case, there are many details to think through. Is an equitable outcome a change in Ms. Grady's policy, or might such a change actually affect Samantha adversely, unintentionally demonstrating low expectations?

Second, remember to *think both immediate term and long term*. What can be resolved right now, on the spot, and what will equity look like once it is resolved? You might decide, for example, that Ms. Grady needs to find a different strategy *right now* to communicate with Samantha. You might consider other stakeholders, such as Samantha's classmates, and an opportunity, like the chance to engage them, many of whom likely share challenges similar to Samantha's challenges, in a conversation about socioeconomic class. Look, too, to the long term. Perhaps an equitable outcome would be professional development on socioeconomic issues for the teachers at Samantha's school or a strengthened relationship between Ms. Grady and Samantha's parents.

Finally, *be specific*. Identify very specific, on-the-ground outcomes. How, specifically, will things be different in that classroom and school if we commit to resolving the issue and all its complexities equitably?

Step 5: Brainstorm Immediate-Term Responses

Now that you have some equitable outcomes in mind, it is time to begin brainstorming strategies to get us there. What are some of the things you might do *right now*, if you were in Ms. Grady's shoes, to achieve those outcomes? This is a brainstorm, remember, so do not overthink. Focus on using the understandings that you've developed in Steps 1 through 4 and, of course, your own experience and expertise, and make a list. You'll have an opportunity later, in Step 7, to craft your ideas into a more formal plan of action.

All we are doing here is making a list. It's an informed list, based on all the work we have been doing in the previous steps. But it is still just a list.

Step 6: Brainstorm Longer-Term Policy and Practice Adjustments

In Step 6 we turn to longer-term strategies, often for more substantive change. This is where we might brainstorm ways to bolster awareness about the sorts of challenges Samantha faces throughout the school, if that is one of our equitable outcomes. It is where we focus on things such as institutional culture, school-wide practices, or even district policy, if we believe they need to be altered in order to achieve our equitable outcomes.

Here, again, we're brainstorming. Try not to self-censor. Just focus on recording whatever ideas come to mind based on Steps 1 through 5.

Step 7: Craft a Plan of Action

During this, the final step, we craft our brainstorms into a set of specific actions that will result in the equitable outcomes we imagined in Step 5. What would you do, if you were in Ms. Grady's shoes, in the immediate term? What would you do that might be a little longer term? How would you respond in order to ensure, to the best of your knowledge and power, equity for everybody involved?

A Few Final Thoughts

We recognize, of course, that in the heat of the moment we do not always have time to sit down and think through the seven steps of a case analysis process. The point is not to memorize these steps. Instead, the idea is to use them to practice our equity literacy skills by reflecting on classroom situations through a diversity and social justice lens. Use them to practice grappling with the nuances and complexities inherent in any interaction within a roomful of people with different aspirations and gifts and challenges. For additional guidance, refer to the "Points for Consideration" included with each case. These points offer valuable insight that might otherwise be missed when analyzing a case. Practice enough, and that equity view will become second nature. We begin to see the nuances and complexities that previously might have been invisible, or at least a little hazy, to us.

3

CASES ON SOCIOECONOMIC STATUS

CASE 3.1: CHOCOLATE BAR FUNDRAISER

For years the Parent Teacher Association (PTA) at Broadway Middle School had organized a variety of fundraisers in attempts to defray the effects of budget cuts or to raise money so that the band or student clubs could participate in out-of-town competitions. Often the fundraisers revolved around students selling something—usually chocolate bars. There were a half-dozen or so different companies that worked with schools on these sorts of fundraisers, providing the chocolate bars and organizing a contest to reward students who sold the most goods with passes to theme parks and other prizes. It had been an easy and effective way to raise money and many of the students enjoyed it.

So at the first PTA meeting of the new school year, when Ms. Alexander, the mother of a Broadway student and a regular attendee of PTA meetings, raised a concern about its plan to run such a fundraiser, several other teachers and parents were surprised. "We've been doing this for years," Ms. Terry, the PTA president, said, "and nobody's ever had a problem with it. What are your concerns, exactly?"

Ms. Alexander, a single mother who struggled financially despite working two jobs, had started attending PTA meetings because she was concerned about school budget cuts and how they were affecting her son. "This school isn't like it used to be," she responded, "when most of the students were from well-to-do families. There are more and more kids at this school like my son, whose families and neighbors can't afford to buy a bunch of candy bars. It's embarrassing, with other students talking about how much of that stuff they've sold to their own parents."

Ms. Terry nodded sympathetically, then asked the group whether anybody else had concerns about the chocolate bar fundraiser. Following a brief silence Mr. Cuertas, whose daughter attended Broadway and who usually remained very quiet during the meetings, raised his hand shyly. "I share the concern about some students being set up to feel embarrassed by this kind of fundraiser. My daughter felt terrible last year when she wasn't able to sell very many candy bars. Anyway, I don't think we should depend on middle school kids to sell stuff in order to raise money for school-related activities."

"I agree," said Ms. Alexander. "When are we going to talk about some of these bigger problems?"

Ms. Terry was aware of and sensitive to the growing numbers of low-income students attending Broadway. She had made what she considered to be a great effort in trying to increase PTA participation among lower-income parents and guardians. She and other PTA officers had sent postcards and placed phone calls to almost every family and made a special point to reach out to the families whom they knew were struggling financially. It was important, she believed, to have their voices in the PTA meetings. These efforts helped to increase participation at PTA meetings. Unfortunately, as far as she could tell, Ms. Alexander and Mr. Cuertas were the only two lower-income parents out of the 20 or so people attending the meeting that night. She appreciated Ms. Alexander and Mr. Cuertas speaking up, but was worried about how other people at the meeting might respond.

Before Ms. Terry could respond to Ms. Alexander and Mr. Cuertas, Ms. Plumlee, sounding a bit annoyed, said, "So, we're not going to let any students do this fundraiser because a few kids might feel bad? Bottom line is that we need extra money and this type of fundraiser has worked well for us in the past."

Mr. Winterstein agreed, adding, "My son sold the second most chocolate bars last year. He did this by working hard, going door to door in several neighborhoods, and emailing every family friend and relative. I really think if these kids just buckled down and worked a little harder, they could sell just as many chocolate bars as my son sold."

"Why don't we just take a vote?" Ms. Plumlee asked. "Isn't that what we normally do when we don't agree on something?"

Ms. Alexander responded, "I don't think you are hearing what I am saying. This activity alienates families like mine."

"Well," Ms. Plumlee answered, "if those families care so much, maybe they should come to these meetings, but they don't come, even after the outreach we did. Now, how about that vote?"

Ms. Plumlee was correct that the group usually voted on issues on which they did not reach a consensus. She called for a vote, which meant that, technically speaking, Ms. Terry was supposed to facilitate a vote. She hesitated, however, empathizing with Ms. Alexander and Mr. Cuertas and feeling that their concerns had not been resolved.

Questions

1 What are the equity implications of fundraisers that require students to sell items such as chocolate bars? Do you agree with Ms. Alexander's concerns about how these fundraisers can alienate low-income students? Why or why not?

2 If the PTA members are intent on raising funds to support student activities or make up for budget cuts, what are some ways in which they can do so that might not require students to compete with each other? How else might the PTA go about addressing the lack of funding for student activities?

3 Ms. Terry knew that the concerns raised by Ms. Alexander and Mr. Cuertas would be drowned out by the voices of other meeting attendees who saw the chocolate bar fundraiser as a school tradition. Can you think of other examples of school traditions that, despite being supported by many people, are biased against or inequitable toward some students and families?

4 How would you respond to Ms. Plumlee's request for a vote if you were Ms. Terry?

Turn to page 127 to view the Points for Consideration for this case.

CASE 3.2: A CLASS LESSON IN ETIQUETTE

Mr. Peyton liked to try new and interesting lessons with his eighth grade students, especially when they involved life skills. Students appreciated him as somebody who always tried to make what they were learning relevant to their lives. So when he saw a story on the local news about Cynthia Hollingsworth, a woman who was doing a residency at a nearby school teaching students dining etiquette, and learned that those students enjoyed her etiquette workshops, he decided to invite her to work with one of his classes.

Mr. Peyton noted that the students in the news story came predominantly from affluent white families, a big difference from his racially diverse classes with many recent immigrants, most of whom were from low-income and working-class families. Because of his school's demographics, he wondered whether he could find a grant to pay for this unique learning experience. He approached his principal who, as it turned out, was friends with Ms. Hollingsworth. After several phone conversations, Ms. Hollingsworth offered to do an abbreviated two-hour version of her residency at no charge for Mr. Peyton's class.

Full of enthusiasm about the idea of providing what would be a new experience for many of his students, Mr. Peyton shared the news with his class. He was pleased when they responded with a bevy of questions and comments about the relevance of the workshop to their lives. "Mr. P.," Kevin, one of his lower-income students, remarked, "you're always telling us how the stuff we learn can be used in the real world. I don't think this is real world learning for us because we'll probably never be invited to a fancy event."

Mr. Peyton thought for a moment. He genuinely wanted his students to see the real world relevance of the upcoming experience. Then he replied, "You never know when these skills will come in handy. The important thing is that you have the chance to learn behaviors that other young people are learning or already know, and we should take advantage of the opportunity." His students seemed satisfied with this response and curious about the prospect of having a guest teacher.

Several days before her visit, Mr. Peyton met Ms. Hollingsworth and briefly described the demographics of his class. "Demographics don't matter at all," she explained, "because all students can be taught dining etiquette and social graces the same way." Her confidence reassured Mr. Peyton, renewing his enthusiasm about bringing this experience to his students.

His feelings were affirmed again the day of Ms. Hollingsworth's visit when, several minutes into the lesson, he observed his students listening eagerly. However, when the time came for students to apply what they had learned, he noticed Ms. Hollingsworth becoming impatient with students who were having a hard time remembering what she had taught them. He noticed, for instance, that after Ms. Hollingsworth twice explained the correct placement of silverware at the dinner table and the order in which the utensils were meant to be used, a few students were unable to demonstrate the placement and explain the order back to her.

Ms. Hollingsworth decided to move on, but she first pointed out that placement settings are basic knowledge that "everybody needs to know. Otherwise," she explained, "you might find yourself in an embarrassing situation."

Later in the lesson, during a discussion on the etiquette of eating, Ms. Hollingsworth reprimanded two students who were eating pieces of diced fruit with their hands. "It's simply not acceptable," she stated.

Mr. Peyton noticed that several students were losing interest in the lesson and not paying attention. When he asked them to pay attention, Tanya, one of his more vocal students, responded, "No thank you. This lady is teaching us to act snooty, and that's not something I want to learn."

Mr. Peyton knew he needed to use this situation as a learning opportunity. Tanya's comment was disrespectful, he thought. But more importantly, he wanted his students to recognize the importance of what they were learning and to realize how these social skills could pay off for them later in life.

Why, he wondered, couldn't his students embrace this opportunity and show Ms. Hollingsworth that they were able to learn what she was teaching just like the students in the other school?

Questions

1 Why might Mr. Peyton's students have questioned whether a workshop on dining etiquette was relevant to their lives? Did

Mr. Peyton respond to Kevin's remark in a constructive way? Why or why not?

2 Mr. Peyton was mindful enough to meet with Ms. Hollingsworth prior to her visit. How, if at all, could he have prepared Ms. Hollingsworth for her visit, knowing that she previously had worked with a much more privileged group of students?

3 Why might Tanya have responded the way she responded? In what ways might her response be connected to Ms. Hollingsworth's approach to teaching etiquette?

4 If you were Mr. Peyton, what would you do to turn this tense situation into a learning opportunity for the students and, perhaps, for Ms. Hollingsworth?

Turn to page 128 to view the Points for Consideration for this case.

CASE 3.3: STUDENT PROTEST

Melody Yazzie and Javier Esposito, both seniors at North Shore High School, had attended Burlington County Public Schools (BCPS) since kindergarten. They went to elementary and middle school together, too, at the lowest-income schools in the district. During their years in the BCPS system, they had seen growing class sizes, a heightened focus on high-stakes testing, and the withering away of music and arts programs in their schools, issues that did not seem to plague the wealthier schools in the district.

Several years earlier, as part of a project for civics class, Melody and Javier attempted to organize a peaceful protest against deteriorating conditions at North Shore. Their teacher, Ms. Terry, was a strong advocate for civic engagement. "It's our duty," she always said, "to change the things that need changing." She ended almost every class with what she called a "Now What Popcorn." Students brainstormed what they could do to create a better world based on what they were studying in class. In one of the final assignments of the school year, she asked her students to craft their brainstorms into a plan of action. "Pick one social issue and, in pairs, propose a plan for creating a better world." Melody and Javier were not satisfied with *proposing* a plan. They wanted to experience protesting, but Ms. Terry quashed the idea. "I love your spirit," she said, "but I don't want you two getting into trouble."

Now, two years later, news began circulating that BCPS intended to close North Shore. The district had been losing students for years and, under state pressure, decided to consolidate schools. North Shore, which had the lowest test scores among the district's high schools, also had failed to make the requisite Annual Yearly Progress for the past three years. It was first on the chopping block.

Teachers received a memo insisting that they not speak to the students about the planned closure until the district knew how it would redistribute them into other schools. Still, there was a lot of chatter, as the situation was all over the local news. Many students were angry. They were sure this wouldn't happen to a school full of wealthier students.

Melody and Javier decided it was time to organize that protest they started planning a few years earlier. Their first step was to ask Ms. Terry for support. "I'm not supposed to talk about this," she said, "but I suggest that you do a little research. Find out what sorts of protests students have done in other districts. Surround yourself with other people who feel like you do. Don't try to do this on your own."

They followed her advice. They invited a group of student leaders and friends to a meeting outside of school. "We have to do something!" Melody insisted.

"The question is, what should we do?" Javier asked.

The students decided that they would divide into groups, each taking on a specific task. Melody and Javier would learn as much as they could about student protests. Two of their peers would read all of the news stories they could find about school closures and how they affect local communities. Others would try to drum up interest among other students. They would meet again in a few days.

When they did meet again they decided they would organize a student walkout, encouraging every student who was upset about the school closure to peacefully leave the school at a predetermined time. They would march a couple of blocks, then line the boulevard, the busiest street in town, holding signs and chanting their displeasure. They would gather that weekend to make the signs. In the meantime their most important task was to spread the word about the walkout and to remind everybody that it would be a *peaceful* protest. "Make sure to tell everyone, no cursing or violence," Melody told the group.

"That's right. We don't want to give anybody a reason to blow us off," Javier added.

They scheduled the walkout for the following Wednesday at 10 a.m. Some teachers urged the students not to continue with their plan, but many others were supportive, even if quietly so. A few teachers, including Ms. Terry, planned to join the walkout.

When Javier saw Melody the morning of the walkout he asked whether she noticed the extra police presence inside and outside of the building. "How could I miss it?" she answered.

Ms. Terry noticed it, too, and it frightened her. She knew the students had their plan together. They would walk out peacefully; no cursing, no violence. But she worried that the police presence would elevate tensions. She knew they were there to scare the students into canceling the walkout, and she knew that was exactly the wrong approach to take with youth who experienced slight after slight in their educational lives. As she sat at her desk wondering what to do, Javier and Melody appeared at her classroom door.

Questions

1 Do you agree with the district's decision to ask teachers not to speak with students about the school consolidation plan while district administrators decided where they would send the students the following year? Why or why not?

2 If you were Ms. Terry, and Melody and Javier approached you for advice about how to funnel their frustrations into positive action, what would you have suggested they do? How involved in their plans would you want to be? What repercussions could exist for your decision if you chose to get involved?

3 Do you agree with Ms. Terry that an increased police presence was a bad strategy? Why or why not?

4 School closings can have detrimental effects on local communities. Why might school closures in low-income areas have

especially detrimental effects on the students and families in those communities?

Turn to page 129 to view the Points for Consideration for this case.

CASE 3.4: HIGH EXPECTATIONS OR UNREALISTIC GOALS?

Ms. Sutter was in the middle of her first year teaching sixth grade at Pinewood Elementary School when she decided to form an after-school club for students who could become the first people in their families to attend college. She came to see a need for such a group as she noticed that many of her students lacked knowledge about post-secondary education. Although many of their parents encouraged them to think about college, her students did not have the same opportunities as some of their peers to see a college campus or hear about higher education options.

The school was located close to several colleges and even a world-renowned university, but only a few of Ms. Sutter's students saw those institutions' potential relevance to their own futures. Ms. Sutter, on the other hand, had fond memories of the friendly rivalry between her parents when they discussed their *alma maters*. At an early age she understood that there was no question about *whether* she would pursue higher education; rather, the question was *where* she would earn her degree.

Ms. Sutter proposed the new club at a staff meeting. Some teachers thought it was unnecessary, but several others were excited and offered their support. A major point of discussion was the club's grade range. Should it be open to all students from kindergarten through sixth grade or limited to higher grade levels?

Ms. Bates, a second grade teacher, commented, "Experience tells me that sixth grade is too early to start talking to *these* kids about college. It's way over their heads."

Another teacher, Ms. Clark, added, "Families in our school will enroll their children in any free after-school program just to keep them busy. You'll be swamped and end up spending more time on discipline than on college. Limit it to sixth graders." Many teachers nodded in agreement.

Ms. Sutter listened carefully to the suggestions and although she disagreed with her peers' opinions, she reluctantly agreed to offer the club exclusively to sixth graders.

Several months later, Ms. Sutter paused during her "College Club" meeting to marvel at how well it was going. Over half of the sixth graders attended regularly. Many parents and guardians would arrive before pick-up time to join the lively discussions about college life. The students even created a map, which was hung in the front office, showing all of the colleges and universities that the school's teachers had attended. It seemed everybody was impressed with the students' enthusiasm and willingness to do additional work.

As a year-end celebration for club members, Ms. Sutter scheduled a Saturday field trip to the renowned local university, which would include a guided tour and lunch. When they arrived on the campus she asked the students to wait outside the admissions office while she went in to notify the receptionist that the group had arrived. Because it was a weekend, the office was crowded with high school students and their families, all awaiting their tours. After speaking with the receptionist Ms. Sutter was shocked to learn that their assigned tour guide had called in sick and that, as a result, her group would need to conduct a self-guided tour.

"But I didn't even attend this university! I can't give them an adequate tour. Why not just let us join another group?" she implored.

"I'm sorry, but our guides are prioritized for the high school students," the receptionist responded. As Ms. Sutter continued to plead the club's case, she was approached by the director of admissions, Mr. Stein.

"Can I help you?" he asked warmly.

"Yes, thank you!" responded Ms. Sutter, hopeful that he would secure a tour guide for the group. "I have a group of sixth graders here, potential first-generation college students," she said, before explaining the purpose of the club and how excited the students were about the tour.

Mr. Stein looked around the crowded room and asked Ms. Sutter to step into his office. *Wonderful!* thought Ms. Sutter. *Maybe he'll be the person who gives us a tour.*

Instead Mr. Stein said, "I'm sorry that a tour guide is unavailable. We do our best to avoid these situations, but I have students waiting in the other room who are credible applicants. Unfortunately, I can't compromise their interest by prioritizing sixth graders ahead of them." He paused briefly before adding, "Frankly, I worry that you're getting your students excited about a place they probably will never be able to attend. Perhaps you should be touring a community college or trade school."

With this, he opened his office door, inviting Ms. Sutter to leave so that he could attend to the families in the lobby. Ms. Sutter glanced through a window and saw her students waiting patiently for their tour. She fought back tears as she contemplated what to tell them and how to address Mr. Stein's prejudiced comments.

Questions

1 What advice would you have given Ms. Sutter when she was deciding which students should be permitted to participate in the club?

2 Ms. Sutter heard from multiple people, including Mr. Stein, that it was unnecessary to discuss post-secondary options with her students. To what extent, if at all, do you agree with this sentiment?

3 Mr. Stein expressed his concern about Ms. Sutter creating false excitement about a prestigious university. How would you have responded to Mr. Stein's comments?

Turn to page 130 to view the Points for Consideration for this case.

4

CASES ON RELIGION

CASE 4.1: THE WINTER PARTY

One evening in early December, several third grade teachers at Chavez Elementary School joined a group of their students' parents after school to plan the upcoming Winter Party. The Winter Party was an annual tradition at the school, always occurring the day before winter break toward the end of December. Teachers at Chavez typically planned the party individually, with separate parties in each classroom. This year, though, the third grade teachers decided to facilitate community-building among their students by having all of them cele-brate together. Stations involving some sort of craft or game would be set up in every classroom, allowing students to rotate among the rooms, and each station would be led by parent volunteers. Rather than generating ideas on their own and assigning volunteers, the teachers invited all of their students' parents and guardians to the meeting to help brainstorm fun party activities.

Once several parents and guardians arrived, the teachers explained the party format and asked for ideas. The parents obliged, sharing a variety of possibilities. One recommended a station where students could decorate paper Christmas trees. Another suggested a station where students could pin tails on reindeer, eliciting excited agreement among other attendees. A third parent suggested, "How about a game in which the kids identify the missing words in popular Christmas carols?"

As the meeting progressed, the group started to identify adults willing to lead each station activity. Ms. Mahdi, whose children were new to the school, was happy to volunteer and was asked to lead the Christmas carol game. She agreed, but then joked that she might not be the best person for that particular station since her family does not celebrate Christmas. "Also," she added, "I have not been in this country long enough to be familiar with the popular songs. I will need a sheet of answers too."

Ms. Madhi's statement prompted Mr. Olson, whose stepson attended the school, to scan the list of activities more closely. "Wait a minute," he said. "Did anybody notice that these are all Christmas activities?" He suggested adding a station related to Hanukkah, such as a dreidel craft. Other parents and guardians nodded their agreement and praised Mr. Olson for trying to make the event more inclusive.

"What about a game or project to represent Kwanzaa?" another parent asked. "Maybe I can find something on the Internet."

Hearing this, Ms. Mahdi suggested not having any activities at the party related to religious celebrations. "I thought this was supposed to be a *winter* party," she said. Several parents opposed this suggestion, explaining that children enjoy Christmas-themed activities.

"We don't see these activities as *religious*," Ms. Tyler said, looking at Ms. Mahdi. "It's really more cultural, more American, than religious."

Sensing the growing tension in the room, Mr. Smithson, another of the parents, reminded the group that the Fall Party in October was based mostly on Halloween, instead of seasonal activities. "Maybe there's some confusion with the name," he said. "Why don't we call it a *Holiday Party* and celebrate *all* of the holidays? Can we do that?" he asked the teachers.

One of the teachers, Ms. Tate, replied that Chavez's principal suggested at a staff meeting several years ago that the event should be called a *Winter Party*. "That is how it appears on the school calendar," she explained, "even though most of the activities in the classrooms still relate to Christmas." After this statement, Ms. Tate realized she was growing concerned that this year's Winter Party would again be a Christmas Party with a couple of token non-Christmas activities thrown in.

Ms. Dyce interjected, "Well, nobody raised any concerns in the past. It sounds like we have no shortage of ideas. Why don't we just write them all down and then take a vote?" She began making a list of suggested activities on the whiteboard.

As she wrote, a parent who, until that point, had been fairly quiet complained, "I think we are trying too hard to be politically correct. These are *third* graders. It's no big deal to do some Christmas-related activities as long as we also have some other activities like snowmen and dreidels. It's OK if students don't celebrate Christmas at home because they see it everywhere in public anyway."

Ms. Tate was pleased that the parents and guardians were taking ownership of the party, but worried that this conversation might alienate some of them and make some of the teachers feel defensive. She also knew that *most* of the people at the meeting did not see a problem with the heavy Christmas theme, despite religious diversity among their students.

She wondered whether she should step in and reiterate the spirit of the principal's policy. *Maybe I should be even more direct and* insist *that we remove every reference to religious holidays*, she thought. On the other hand, all of these parents and guardians had shown up. They were involved and engaged. They were volunteers. The last thing she wanted to do was to alienate volunteers! She knew she had to do something, though, and soon.

Questions

1   Mr. Smithson suggested that they call the event a Holiday Party and try to include "all of the holidays." What do you think he meant by "all of the holidays"? Do you think his suggestion is a good one? Why or why not?

2   What kind of privilege can be made manifest when teachers and schools turn decision-making over to parents? How can teachers and schools encourage parent engagement and empowerment and ensure that multiple voices and viewpoints are heard?

3   What role can teachers play in either ensuring equity or enshrining privilege in the ways that they communicate with or "hear" from different parents? How can a teacher's unaddressed biases affect who is truly "heard"?

4 If you were in Ms. Tate's shoes, would you encourage the group to refocus its efforts on a *winter* theme instead of a holiday theme, or wait until next year and be more proactive with anticipating the issue?

Turn to page 131 to view the Points for Consideration for this case.

CASE 4.2: CHRISTMAS LIGHTS?

While driving to a store in an unfamiliar area after work one October evening, Ms. Bren, a seventh grade teacher at Franklin Middle School, noticed a few houses in the neighborhood behind the school with lights of various colors strung around the roof and landscaping. Despite the relatively small number of these houses, Ms. Bren found herself becoming annoyed by the sight of Christmas lights so early in the fall. One house even had a string of lights on the inside of its front window, plugged in and twinkling brightly. *What are these people thinking?* Ms. Bren wondered to herself. *It's not even Halloween yet!*

Upon finding the store, Ms. Bren could not resist sharing what she saw on her drive, so she sent out a tweet: "Just saw homes w/Christmas lights already! Anyone else as annoyed as I am?!" She felt instantly validated when several of her friends responded with similar sentiments.

The next day, as students were filing into their first period class, Ms. Bren stood at the door and greeted everyone cheerfully. One of her students, Juan, who usually wore a perpetual smile, seemed bothered and was unusually quiet when she asked how he was doing. He shrugged as he walked to his seat. *Must have had a not-so good morning*, Ms. Bren thought before heading to her desk.

Moments later her colleague, Mr. Richards, walked into her classroom. "Good morning Ms. Bren," he said. "I saw your tweet yesterday but couldn't respond." He laughed, explaining, "I agree! Displaying Christmas lights before Halloween is a little ridiculous. I don't like putting them up in the cold but there's no way I would consider doing it before Thanksgiving."

Ms. Bren nodded and added, "Thank goodness I'm not the only one who feels that way. People are hanging Christmas lights earlier and earlier every year. Next year we'll start seeing Christmas lights before Labor Day!"

Mr. Richards continued to chuckle and wished Ms. Bren a good day as he left her classroom. Ms. Bren looked at her students, who were all seated awaiting the start of class. She issued her typical morning check-in: "How are you all today?" She noticed that several of her students, including Juan, were unusually quiet and looked a little withdrawn. "Did I miss something this morning?" she asked. "Most of you don't seem to be in your typical joyful moods."

"We're cool, Ms. B" responded Antonio, though Ms. Bren noticed that he avoided eye contact. He then muttered something about a tweet but because she was not sure what he had heard, Ms. Bren chose to ignore his comment. "All right then," she said with a sigh before adding, "You all can inform me of any problems whenever you're ready, but for now you need to wake up so we can have a productive class." She smiled and walked to the front of the classroom to begin her lesson.

Later that day Ms. Wilson, one of Ms. Bren's colleagues, dropped by her classroom.

"Do you have a second?" Ms. Wilson asked.

"Sure," Ms. Bren replied. "What's up?"

"Well," Ms. Wilson began, hesitating slightly, "I just wanted to let you know that I overheard Antonio and several other students talking about a tweet you sent last night. Something about Christmas lights. He seemed upset and Selena said you and Mr. Richards had no business insulting their friend's family, especially since they don't even celebrate Christmas."

Ms. Bren felt sick to her stomach. "Thanks for letting me know," she replied, embarrassed by what she had just learned. As Ms. Wilson walked out of the room, Ms. Bren wondered how her students knew about her tweet and whom else she might have offended. She also wondered if this explained why some students seemed disengaged and did not master the content from her lesson.

Questions

1 What assumptions, if any, did Ms. Bren make as she was driving through the neighborhood close to her school? Why might she be inclined to make these assumptions?

2 What impact might the conversation between Ms. Bren and Mr. Richards have had for the students who were listening and whose families did have lights on their houses? What impact might it have had for students who were listening but who did not have lights on their houses?

3 Should Ms. Bren censor what she communicates through social media because she is a teacher? Why or why not?

Turn to page 132 to view the Points for Consideration for this case.

CASE 4.3: A DIFFERENCE IN PERSPECTIVES

Upon entering his classroom during homeroom period, Mr. Ortiz, an eighth grade teacher, noticed several students crowded around two of their peers, Nikhil and Jasper. They were arguing about something Nikhil was wearing.

Mr. Ortiz asked the students to take their seats and inquired about the conflict. Jasper explained, "Nikhil is wearing a swastika and I don't think it should be at school. It's offensive." Mr. Ortiz glanced at Nikhil but didn't notice anything controversial about his attire. Before he could inquire further, Nikhil looked at Jasper and retorted, "Your ignorance is offensive! I got this from my grandmother."

"Whoa!" Mr. Ortiz replied. "Perhaps someone other than Jasper or Nikhil can explain what's going on here." Madelyn, one of their class-mates, shared her perspective: "Nikhil is wearing a gold chain from his grandmother, and it has a swastika pendant on it. Jasper got upset when he saw it and asked Nikhil why he was wearing a Nazi symbol. Then Nikhil said it's an ancient Hindu symbol or something, but Jasper cut him off and said that it shouldn't be allowed in school because it represents hate." She continued, "I agree with Jasper. It's not cool for Nikhil to wear that."

When Madelyn finished speaking, the students looked to Mr. Ortiz for a response. "May I see your necklace, Nikhil?" he asked. Nikhil pulled the gold chain out from under his t-shirt, revealing a penny-sized pendant that looked like a swastika.

"That was a gift from your grandmother?" asked Mr. Ortiz.

"Yeah," replied Nikhil. "She passed away recently and it was hers. I'm wearing it to honor her."

"You understand that this symbol is offensive to a lot of people, right?" Mr. Ortiz asked.

"Yes, but it's important in my religion. If people learn the deeper history of it, they shouldn't have a problem with me wearing it. It's no different from wearing a cross." After hearing Nikhil's explanation, several students expressed their disagreement.

"OK, OK," said Mr. Ortiz. "Quiet down and remember to raise your hand if you have something to say. This is a longer discussion than we have time to have today, as you need to get to your first period classes. We'll discuss it tomorrow, I assure you, and we'll find some resolution then."

"That's fine with me," responded Jasper. "But Nikhil should take it off until then." This comment started another commotion, leading Mr. Ortiz to believe he needed to resolve the matter immediately. As he was thinking about what to say, he saw Madelyn waving her hand in the air, eager to share something.

"Yes, Madelyn?" he asked.

"Nikhil is telling the truth," Madelyn shared. "I just looked it up on my phone and that *is* an ancient Hindu symbol. Looks like it's been used in *a lot* of religions and cultures before it became a Nazi symbol. Actually, the one used by the Nazis looks a little different from what Nikhil is wearing."

"*Of course* I'm telling the truth," Nikhil responded, sounding defensive. "This chain means a lot to me and I'm not taking it off just because people are ignorant."

Mr. Ortiz didn't know anything about the history of the swastika, but he did know that Nikhil's necklace could be disruptive to some students. Although learning more about it would be a great educational opportunity, he worried it would be impossible for the conversation to reach everyone in the school and he did not want to deal with additional disruptions. He proposed a solution to Nikhil, hoping he would agree.

"You are right about our ignorance, Nikhil," he said, "but you can't go around educating everyone who sees you wearing it and you can't just call everybody ignorant. We have to consider the disruption your necklace is causing, and since most people seem to think of it as symbol of hate, I don't think you should wear it in school. Perhaps you can still honor your grandmother by wearing it at home."

"No," responded Nikhil, "I don't think it's fair that other students can display their religious symbols and I can't. I'm not taking it off."

Mr. Ortiz replied, "OK, I'll stop by the principal's office later today to see what she has to say. Until then, you can wear the necklace, but please keep it under your shirt."

The bell rang and the students headed to their first period classes. Mr. Ortiz knew it would be only a matter of hours before everyone in the school had learned about Nikhil's chain. *We need to figure this out quickly*, he thought.

Questions

1 To what extent, if at all, was Mr. Ortiz's suggestion for Nikhil to wear the charm at home a fair compromise?

2 Nikhil believes it is unjust to allow other students to display their religion symbols while he is not allowed to do the same. Do you agree? Why or why not?

3 This conflict arises during homeroom and it appears as though Mr. Ortiz is concerned about the lack of time he has to address it. If you were Mr. Ortiz, how would you address the situation given the limited time?

4 Should Mr. Ortiz and other educators at the school educate the student body about the history of this religious symbol so that Nikhil can continue wearing the charm? How might the religious identities of people in the school and broader community influence your response?

Turn to page 133 to view the Points for Consideration for this case.

CASE 4.4: ISLAMOPHOBIC READ-ALOUD

Ms. McGrath, a language arts and journalism teacher at Grove High School, was determined to help her journalism students learn how to write thoughtfully about complex social issues. Some were most interested in writing about sports or popular culture, which they eventually would have the opportunity to do in her class, but only after they had developed their skills writing about the political controversies of the day. She raised a few eyebrows among her colleagues and her students' parents for encouraging students to write about everything from gay marriage to gun control. However, she was very skilled at keeping her own views on these issues to herself, so although her teaching elicited an occasional complaint, her principal was supportive and the tension always waned fairly quickly.

Ms. McGrath also believed that students interested in journalism needed to stay apprised of current events. She would start every class period with a question: "What's new today?" Students were assessed, in part, on how well they kept up with the news.

Grove was a predominantly Christian and upper middle-class school near Washington, D.C. During the past five or six years a small but growing population of Muslim students, mostly children of diplomats, also from upper middle-class families, had started attending the school. Ms. McGrath knew that some of the Muslim students had experienced bullying and teasing, but for the most part, at least in her classes, everybody got along well. Students knew that she would not tolerate name-calling or prejudiced jokes. Two students in her journalism class were Muslim.

A few weeks into the new school year, with the anniversary of the September 11, 2001 attacks on the World Trade Center and the Pentagon approaching, her students began talking about news stories commemorating the event. Sensitive to the likelihood that some of her students' families had been directly affected by the attacks given Grove High School's close proximity to the Pentagon, Ms. McGrath encouraged their curiosity and decided to develop a couple of writing activities about the topic.

A few days before the anniversary, Ms. McGrath asked her students, as she often did, to do a free write. "Remember the rules of our free writes," she said. "Don't overthink. Write whatever comes to your mind." Then she gave them their free write prompt: "What, in your opinion, has been the impact of the events of September 11, 2001 on U.S. culture?" She instructed the students, "You have five minutes to write."

After five minutes she asked for volunteers to read all or part of their free writes to the class. "We can learn as much about our writing by hearing it as we can by reading it silently," she reminded them. After the requisite wait time, Ms. McGrath noticed that George, an outspoken junior who was known for frequently referencing his Christian faith in classes, was the only student volunteering. She reluctantly looked at him and nodded, and he stood up to read his free write.

"I believe most people are good people," he read, "but I believe the Muslim religion is immoral. 9/11 was a tragedy brought to this country by an immoral religion. It changed everything from how we travel to who we allow into our country." Ms. McGrath considered interrupting George's reading at this point, but one week earlier, when they did their first share-alouds of the semester, she set the ground rule, *we listen carefully and mindfully, without interrupting.* She felt stuck. George continued, "But as a Christian, what's most important to me is that the attacks helped us remember how important it is for the U.S. to be a Christian nation. That will turn out to be a good thing for American culture."

George bowed playfully and sat down. Ms. McGrath, scanning the room, was surprised to see several students nodding in agreement. Hasina, one of her Muslim students, stared down at her desk. Essam, the other Muslim student, looked as though he wanted to say something then looked at Ms. McGrath as if to say, "Are you going to respond to that?"

Ms. McGrath knew she needed to respond, but she was not sure how to do so.

Questions

1   Should Ms. McGrath have interrupted George's reading despite her own ground rule? Why or why not? If she had decided to interrupt his reading, how might she have addressed his anti-Muslim sentiments in an effective way?

2   Ms. McGrath had developed a reputation for being balanced on controversial issues, which is part of what allowed her to continue to engage students around those issues despite the occasional

complaint. What was her responsibility in this scenario? Should she have taken a stand against George's prejudice? Why or why not?

3 What are the implications of how Ms. McGrath responds to George's reading for Hasina and Essam? What are the implications for the other students?

Turn to page 134 to view the Points for Consideration for this case.

5

CASES ON ETHNICITY AND CULTURE

CASE 5.1: GENERALIZATIONS ON DISPLAY

Ms. Whitney, an eighth grade mathematics teacher, wandered the halls of Crestwood Elementary School, eagerly awaiting the end of her daughter Jessica's basketball practice. In order to pass the time she decided to look at the posters of students' work displayed outside one of the fifth grade classrooms. Based on what she saw in the posters' content, she figured that each student had chosen a country to study and then made a poster with photos and interesting information about it.

Ms. Whitney was taken aback when she saw this sentence on one of the posters: "People in Mexico are poor so they want to come to the United States." She was dismayed by the overgeneralization and the fact that it was displayed for everybody to read. As she scanned the other projects, she found herself equally dismayed by other generalizations she found. In addition to the misinformation, she noticed that some students were not consistent with their verb tenses, which resulted in inaccurate statements. One student, Michael, had chosen Japan for his project. He had included a paragraph about World War II in the corner of the poster. One of his sentences read, "Japanese people in America are in special camps because Japan was at war with the United States." Ms. Whitney could not believe what she had just read. *How can this type of work be hung in the hallways for others to read?*, she wondered.

Just then Ms. Whitney's daughter ran up to her and announced that she was finished with practice. Because Crestwood was in her daughter's district, but not the school her daughter attended, Ms. Whitney made a mental note of the name of the teacher, Ms. Lewis, whose class had made the posters. She decided to send Ms. Lewis an email expressing her concerns. Crestwood had a large population of recent immigrant students, so she felt especially obligated to speak up.

That night Ms. Whitney drafted an email and read it several times to ensure that she sounded constructive rather than critical. After sending the email, she wondered whether Ms. Lewis simply had not checked all of the projects before displaying them. She hoped the situation could be fixed easily.

The next morning, Ms. Whitney was pleased to see a response. After reading the email, however, she again felt dismayed. Ms. Lewis thanked Ms. Whitney for taking the time to contact her and said that the posters had been on display for several weeks. Nobody else had complained, she noted, and agreed that she should change the verb tense on the Japan poster before adding that, because the sentence was written under a section entitled World War II, "the reader really should assume it was meant to be past tense." She continued, "As for the generalizations, the students did their own research. These generalizations are not completely inaccurate. Perhaps because you teach at a junior high school, you have more of a critical eye than I do. These, after all, are only fifth graders."

Ms. Whitney was not sure how to respond. She felt that Ms. Lewis had dismissed her concerns and worried that Ms. Lewis did not mention any plans to discuss the generalizations with her students. Still feeling concerned, Ms. Whitney drafted an email to the principal of Crestwood about the matter, but then decided not to send it, fearing that Ms. Lewis would get in trouble. *Maybe the posters will be removed soon*, she thought, *before any harm is done*.

The following week, Jessica once again had basketball practice at Crestwood. After taking her to the gymnasium, Ms. Whitney wandered to the fifth grade hallway to see whether the posters were still displayed. To her disappointment, they remained on display, and no changes had been made to the Japan poster.

She noticed that Ms. Lewis was still in the classroom, so she introduced herself. Ms. Lewis, realizing that she had not edited the verb tense on the Japan poster, apologized and said that she had intended to do so but had forgotten. She then pointed to a pile of posters illustrating flowers that the students had drawn in art class. "I was just about to replace the country posters with these," she explained. "They should be much less controversial for you," she added with a friendly laugh.

Ms. Whitney paused, wondering whether she should laugh in polite response or express her frustrations about feeling dismissed or about the fact that Ms. Lewis's students were learning and conveying misinformation. She also wondered whether any students or parents saw the posters and felt offended, or whether other staff noticed these issues.

She decided she should say something about her concerns. The question was, what should she say and how should she say it?

Questions

1 Do you believe that Ms. Whitney had an obligation to share her concerns with Ms. Lewis despite the fact that Crestwood was neither her workplace nor her daughter's school?

2 If you were Ms. Whitney, how would you respond to Ms. Lewis at the end of this case? How, if at all, would you have responded differently after the email response from Ms. Lewis earlier in the case?

3 If these posters had been displayed in a classroom instead of a public hallway, would your response to the previous two questions change? Would your response change depending on the grade level of the students? If so, how?

4 If Ms. Lewis decided she did need to help her students understand the generalizations on their posters and how those generalizations might be offensive, how would you recommend she go about doing so?

Turn to page 134 to view the Points for Consideration for this case.

CASE 5.2: NOT TIME FOR STORIES

Ms. Ward was a big fan of geography. As a second grade teacher, she inspired and motivated her students by telling them that they were learning material, such as states and capitals, which was typically reserved for fourth and fifth graders.

The first unit that Ms. Ward planned for the new school year focused on California. Although Roosevelt Elementary School, where Ms. Ward taught, was located in the Midwest, she thought it would be a fun state with which to kick off the year. Students at Roosevelt represented a wide range of socioeconomic and racial diversity, but she knew that many of them were interested in ocean beaches. California, in her mind, would fit well with this theme.

In order to kick off the unit, Ms. Ward gathered her students on the carpet and began writing on a flip chart. Several students whispered excitedly as she wrote "California" at the top of the sheet. Although Ms. Ward was happy to hear their excitement, she reminded the students to remain quiet and raise their hands if they had something to say. Immediately, several hands shot up in the air.

"Madelyn," Ms. Ward said, calling on one of her students.

"Are we going to learn about California?" Madelyn asked.

"Yes," the teacher replied. "We will be learning about California in many of our subjects, including math and reading, throughout the week." Students started to chatter excitedly among themselves again, and Ms. Ward reminded them to remain quiet: "I cannot understand you if so many of you are talking at once."

After explaining the unit a little more, Ms. Ward asked her students to raise their hands if they had been to California and to be prepared to tell the class about the state. One boy, DeQuan, raised his hand. When Ms. Ward called on him he said, "A few days ago, I was at my grandmother's house watching television with my little sister, but she was crying so I couldn't hear very well. I told her to be quiet and gave her a toy to play with because the person on TV. . . ."

Ms. Ward interrupted DeQuan and reminded him that the question she had asked was whether anyone had been to California. Growing bothered by the side chatter and DeQuan's indirect answer, she reminded the class that now was not the time for stories.

"Please raise your hand only if you can answer the question," she said. Upon hearing this, DeQuan angrily added under his breath, but loud enough for Ms. Ward and others around him to hear, "But I was saying that the person on TV said the show was sponsored by a company that makes raisins, which are my favorite snack, and that the raisins are made in California!"

Ms. Ward calmly told DeQuan to stop being disrespectful and reminded him that he needed to raise his hand if he had something to say. Attempting to refocus the group, she smiled and asked, "Has anyone been to Hollywood or Disneyland?" In response to this question, Madelyn raised her hand and said, "I have. They are both in California, and it is sunny and warm there. It's also far away because we were on the airplane for a long time."

"You're right," replied Ms. Ward as she wrote "warm" and "sunny" along with the phrase "far from Roosevelt Elementary" on the flip chart.

"Any other words to describe California?" she asked her students. As several others raised their hands, Ms. Ward noticed that DeQuan still looked angry. Anticipating another outburst, Ms. Ward cheerfully said, "DeQuan, please try to compose yourself so that you can remain seated with the group." Hearing this, DeQuan scowled at her, stood up, walked over to his desk, and slouched in his chair.

Oh no, thought Ms. Ward. *He must not have heard me correctly.* Knowing that time was passing quickly and that she needed to get through the lesson, Ms. Ward continued teaching but wondered how she should address DeQuan if his bad mood persisted.

Questions

1 How did Ms. Ward's behavior in this scenario fail to ensure an equitable and just learning environment for the full diversity of her students?

2 What differences can you identify in Madelyn's and DeQuan's responses to their teacher's question? What similarities can you identify?

3 In anticipation of another outburst, Ms. Ward cheerfully gave DeQuan some instructions. What might have caused DeQuan to react the way he did?

4 What long-term effects can manifest if Ms. Ward does not remedy the situation? What advice would you give Ms. Ward in order to re-engage DeQuan?

Turn to page 135 to view the Points for Consideration for this case.

CASE 5.3: INAPPROPRIATE LANGUAGE

Ms. Lindquist, an eleventh grade physical education teacher, tried to encourage students to exercise regularly rather than only doing so while they were in her class. At the beginning of each class period, while students stretched, she liked to ask them what kinds of exercise they had done since their previous day in P. E. The variety of responses, she thought, helped her students to see the many ways in which they could keep their bodies active, whether through organized sports, exercise classes such as yoga, or simple, informal games like catch.

One day, several of her students discussed a soccer match they played the previous evening, but nobody else shared an example of how they had exercised. "Is that all?" Ms. Lindquist asked. "Only the soccer players were active yesterday?" As several students nodded in agreement, Ms. Lindquist called on Devin, who had raised his hand.

"A bunch of us did a Chinese fire drill on the way to the soccer match," he offered, chuckling. "It was a good workout and Simren almost didn't make it back into the car." Several students laughed. Simren added, "Yeah. *That* was a good workout!"

As the laughter continued, Ms. Lindquist wondered how she should respond. As far as she knew none of the students in her class identified ethnically as Chinese. Still, though she did not know the origin of the term "Chinese fire drill," she feared that it could be offensive. She scanned the room, noting that several students were still laughing and a few others looked confused, perhaps not understanding what the students meant by "Chinese fire drill."

As if she had read Ms. Lindquist's mind, another student, Shelly, shouted out, "What is a Chinese fire drill?"

Devin responded, "It's when you're in a car and you stop at a red light. Everyone gets out of the car, runs around it, and switches seats before the light turns green."

"Oh," Shelly replied, looking a little perplexed.

"What do you think about that, Shelly?" Ms. Lindquist asked, hoping to seize the opportunity to engage her students in a conversation about the name of the game. "Do you think that is an offensive name?"

"No," replied Shelly. "I think it sounds dangerous."

As students laughed at Shelly's response, Ms. Lindquist thought, *Well, maybe the students don't see anything wrong with the term.* She wondered whether she should say anything more or continue with the day's lesson.

Before she could decide, another student asked Ms. Lindquist whether she had ever participated in a Chinese fire drill. "Yes, when I was in college," she answered, "but I don't use that term because some people find it derogatory."

To her surprise, her response prompted a lively exchange about a variety of terms and whether they were offensive. Many students shared that as long as people do not *intend* to be offensive by the language they use, other people should not be offended by it.

"The teachers are too sensitive in this school," Simren complained. "I bet you all use terms like 'gay' and 'retarded' and 'Chinese fire drill' when you are with *your* friends, but you tell us we can't use them in school." Several students agreed.

Unsure of where to take the conversation next, Ms. Lindquist regretted saying anything at all about Devin's use of the term "Chinese fire drill." She decided to begin the activity she had planned for the day before the conversation got out of hand.

"All right," she said, "we are going to table this discussion and move on. And for the record, I don't use those terms with my friends."

She blew her whistle, signifying the end of stretching.

Questions

1 When Ms. Lindquist noticed that none of her students seemed to mind the term, should she have let it go? Why might a student who was offended by language such as "Chinese fire drill" have chosen not to speak up about it?

2 How, if at all, should Ms. Lindquist have replied to Simren's comment about teachers in the school being too sensitive?

3 Is a physical education class, in this case, the right context in which to have a conversation about offensive language? Why or why not?

4 Are there terms that are used widely in your school or among your peers whose meanings you do not know but think could be offensive? If so, have you tried to find the terms' meanings?

Turn to page 136 to view the Points for Consideration for this case.

CASE 5.4: MULTICULTURAL DAY PARADE

In an effort to recognize the growing racial and ethnic diversity at Eastern Elementary School, the school's Diversity Committee decided to sponsor Multicultural Day, a day dedicated to celebrating the many cultures represented within the student population. Numerous performers were hired for assemblies and classroom presentations. During the day's feature event, the "Cultural Parade," students were asked to showcase their "ethnic" clothing as they walked through the hallways. In order to prepare for the event, teachers were instructed by the committee to discuss clothing from countries outside the United States with their students and to invite students who had such clothing at home to bring it to school for the parade.

Ms. Morrison, a veteran teacher, was excited about Multicultural Day because she had many students who were immigrants, or whose parents were immigrants, in her fourth grade class. She imagined the day as a fantastic opportunity for those students to be the center of attention and for her other students to learn about their peers' cultures.

A week before the event, Ms. Morrison brought a kilt to class and explained its significance to her students. "This," she said, "represents my Scottish heritage and I am proud to show it to you today." She then asked whether students had special costumes at home that represented their cultures. Several students raised their hands, which prompted Ms. Morrison to discuss the events that were planned for Multicultural Day, including the parade.

Later, the day before the parade, during dismissal, Ms. Morrison announced to her students, "Don't forget to bring your costumes to class tomorrow. We're very excited about Multicultural Day!"

The next day, Ms. Morrison was pleased to see that several of her Hmong and Liberian students came with bags of clothing. Ms. Morrison also noticed that two of her students, Emily and Keisha, also brought clothing and so she walked over to them to inquire about what was in their bags. Emily, a white student, excitedly pulled out her soccer uniform, and Keisha, an African American student, pulled jeans and her favorite sweatshirt out of her bag. Ms. Morrison told the two girls that she appreciated their enthusiasm for Multicultural Day but that they would not be able to walk in the parade and instead could view it with the rest of the class. She explained that what Keisha and Emily brought was everyday clothing rather than clothes that represented their ethnic heritages.

Both girls protested. "This outfit represents my culture," Keisha argued.

Ms. Morrison shared with the girls that she felt terrible about the confusion, but could not allow them to participate. "Maybe next year they'll expand the parade," she said.

After the girls walked away, Ms. Morrison considered changing her mind. She worried, though, that other students or staff would be puzzled by their participation and that Keisha and Emily would be ridiculed for not following directions.

Questions

1 What images come to mind when you hear the term "costume?" How might this word be interpreted by students? In what ways might it be considered demeaning?

2 What are the potential dangers of events such as the Cultural Parade? How might they contribute to students' and teachers' existing stereotypes and biases?

3 People often conflate "culture," "ethnicity," "heritage," "race," and "nationality" or use them interchangeably. How are these concepts different from each other? Is a "Multicultural Day" different than an "International Day"?

4 How might activities that require students to share part of their ethnic heritage alienate students who, like descendants of slaves or adopted children, might not know what their ethnic heritage is?

Turn to page 137 to view the Points for Consideration for this case.

CASE 5.5: A PLACE TO STUDY

It was Back to School Night at Oak Grove Elementary School. As always, Ms. Grady was looking forward to meeting her students' families and setting expectations for the school year. Over the summer she decided that this year she wanted to stress the importance of at-home study habits with her students and that she would introduce her plan at the very beginning of the school year. In order to motivate her students, she purchased a pencil box for each of them to take home. She filled each box with various writing instruments that her students could use to complete their homework.

Many families came to Ms. Grady's classroom during Back to School Night and listened as she explained how important it was for students to have a designated place at home to study quietly and keep learning materials.

One of Ms. Grady's students, Shua, was especially excited about the pencil box. His parents seemed responsive to Ms. Grady's suggestions, nodding as she spoke.

About a month into the school year, Ms. Grady began to notice that Shua was turning in homework with small food stains on it. She also noticed that he was crossing out some answers instead of erasing them. When she asked Shua about this he replied that his siblings also had been using his pencils and pens and that they did not always return them to his pencil box, which was why he had not been using an eraser.

"And the food stains?" Ms. Grady asked. Shua explained that he and his older brother did their homework at the dining room table, sometimes while other people in his family were eating. "My brother remembers doing the same type of homework when he was in my grade," Shua added, "so he helps me sometimes."

Ms. Grady responded that she was sympathetic to Shua's situation and would give him another set of utensils, all labeled with his name so others in his family would know that they belonged to him. "Remember to find a quiet, *separate* place to work where you can keep your school materials instead of working and keeping everything at the dining room table," she told him with a gentle pat on the shoulder. Shua nodded in agreement.

As Shua left the room, Ms. Grady worried about whether he was completing his homework on his own or just recording answers being told to him by his brother. Despite often being stained with food, Shua's work generally was flawless.

A few weeks later, after seeing little change in the condition of Shua's homework, Ms. Grady followed up with him regarding where he was studying and whether his siblings were still using the utensils in his pencil box. Shua, noticeably uncomfortable, replied, "I still work at the table and sometimes they still use my stuff." Ms. Grady thanked Shua for his honesty.

Later, when the school day had ended, she wondered how she should approach Shua's parents at the upcoming parent–teacher conferences. She remembered that they seemed supportive about her expectations that students have a quiet place to study when she discussed them at the Back to School event. If they were supportive in front of her, but did not follow through at home, she worried they also would not be supportive of her other ideas for at-home learning activities. She also wondered whether she should refer Shua's parents to a local agency that could provide donations if the family needed additional school supplies at home, since all of the siblings were using Shua's supplies.

Feeling frustrated about the situation, she packed her things and left for the day.

Questions

1 What outcome was Ms. Grady hoping to achieve by talking about study habits during the Back to School meeting? Do you feel her strategies were useful? Why or why not?

2 Ms. Grady had an expectation for how the pencil case should be used and even gave Shua an additional case to ensure proper use. Was her expectation reasonable? Why or why not?

3 Shua became uncomfortable when his teacher followed up with him about her recommendations. How, if at all, should she have handled this conversation differently?

4 Ms. Grady was feeling frustrated for many reasons and was wondering how she should handle the situation at the upcoming conference, including addressing the homework concerns and suggesting other learning activities. If you were Ms. Grady's co-worker, what advice would you give her?

Turn to page 138 to view the Points for Consideration for this case.

6

CASES ON RACE

CASE 6.1: TASK FORCE

Ms. Diaz, an educational assistant at Pike Elementary School, stopped by the staff lounge before the start of the school day to leave her lunch in the refrigerator. While she was there she overheard a conversation between two teachers regarding an after-school meeting scheduled for later that day. The teachers, Ms. Bayfield and Mr. Dawson, mentioned the importance of the meeting, but they seemed unsure about whether it would fit into their schedules.

Seeing Ms. Diaz, they turned to her and asked whether she was planning to attend the meeting. "I'm sorry," she replied, "but I don't know which meeting you're talking about."

Ms. Bayfield explained that the purpose of the meeting was to create a task force consisting of district administrators, school staff, and parents in order to address some of the pressing issues in the school. "We know we're a good school," she said. "Unfortunately, as you know, our test scores are way below the district average. Plus, we have a huge concentration of students on free and reduced lunch. Now the state department of education is threatening to intervene if we don't raise those test scores."

"Oh, dear," said Ms. Diaz. "I'll be there for sure, but I wish I had known about the meeting earlier."

Mr. Dawson replied, "Well, I heard it's been posted on the district's Web site for the last few weeks and that it was listed under 'volunteer opportunities' in the last newsletter." He added, "We knew about it because it was discussed at the last staff meeting. Hopefully we'll have a good turnout." The bell rang, so Mr. Dawson and Ms. Bayfield headed to their classrooms. Ms. Diaz called home and left a message that she would be home later than usual.

As she headed to the media center later that evening, a few minutes before the meeting was to commence, Ms. Diaz wondered who else would attend. She knew many of the families whose children attended Pike and hoped to see some of the parents and guardians of recent immigrant students and students of color, many of whom had expressed concerns to her about the school's performance. Upon entering the meeting, she saw one parent she recognized, Mr. Webb, and went to sit by him. As people continued to filter into the room, Ms. Diaz realized that she and Mr. Webb were the only people present who were not Pike teachers or administrators or people from the district office.

Also present was a consultant who asked attendees to call him Scott. He started the meeting by outlining a process for creating a plan to address the achievement and demographic concerns, noting that they would develop their plan over the course of four meetings. He thanked the people who were present and encouraged them to speak freely, making a point to say how important it was for everyone's voice to be heard. "The people in this room," he said, "will make significant changes to Pike Elementary School so that *all* students can succeed."

Upon hearing this comment, Mr. Webb leaned over to Ms. Diaz and whispered, "Where are the other parents?" Ms. Diaz shook her head, unsure how to respond. Later, as she began to understand the magnitude of the decisions the task force would make on behalf of the school and the families in the community, she raised her hand to express her concerns. She explained her belief that more parents and guardians, especially those who identified with the groups being discussed by the task force, should be part of the decision-making. Mr. Webb nodded in agreement, but he was the only one to do so.

An attendee from the district office, Mr. Clark, responded, "While it would be good to have more voices here, the reality with most task forces like this one is that parents are simply too busy to attend all the meetings." He added that, in his experience, schools with demographics similar to Pike's, with high numbers of students who qualify for the free and reduced lunch program or high numbers of recent immigrants, typically did not have good parent representation from those groups on decision-making committees.

Scott, feeling a need to reassure Ms. Diaz, added that the task force meeting had been posted on the district's Web site and included in the school newsletter. "All parents," he said, "had various opportunities to learn about the meeting. We need task force members to commit to coming to *all* meetings and that type of commitment just isn't likely for many families. You've raised important concerns, but now we need to work with the people who showed up and utilize their time efficiently. Maybe later we can return to this discussion about how to increase involvement."

Ms. Diaz and Mr. Webb shook their heads, feeling that their concerns were being dismissed and also feeling helpless to do anything else without jeopardizing their own credibility on the task force.

Questions

1 Were the strategies used to announce the meeting to parents and guardians sufficient to ensure adequate representation on the task force? What other strategies, both in terms of announcing the task force and scheduling the first meeting, might have yielded greater attendance by Pike parents and guardians?

2 Scott, the consultant, and a representative from the district each pointed out that consistent attendance at task force meetings was important, even if at the expense of adequate family representation. Do you agree or disagree? Why?

3 Ms. Diaz and Mr. Webb worried that if they pressed the issue of representation, they would jeopardize their credibility with other task force members. In what other contexts might people worry that demanding equity might result in them being viewed as troublemakers and their concerns being dismissed? Have you experienced or witnessed such a situation?

4 Consider the task forces or other decision-making groups at your school. Are the demographics of your student population represented within these groups? If not, how might this be addressed?

Turn to page 139 to view the Points for Consideration for this case.

CASE 6.2: TEACHING RACE WITH *HUCKLEBERRY FINN*

Samuel, one of three African American students in Ms. Kohl's tenth grade language arts class, usually loved discussing literature. A dynamic teacher who actively engaged students, Ms. Kohl enjoyed having them act out the stories they read in order to connect more deeply with characters. Samuel always volunteered to play one of the characters, and he played them with passion.

Ms. Kohl's favorite novel was Mark Twain's *The Adventures of Huckleberry Finn*. So when her students returned to class on Monday after reading its first 50 pages, she couldn't wait to start with a student-led reenactment. "Let's get the words into our shared atmosphere," she was fond of saying.

She was aware, of course, that this approach could be risky with a novel like *Huck Finn*, which was full of racialized language. She considered talking with her students, at the very least, about the use of the n-word in the novel before they read it. But she resisted, concerned that even beginning with that discussion might manipulate the students into a particular view of the book.

Once students were settled into their desks, she asked for volunteers: "Who wants to play a role?" Several students raised their hands but, to Ms. Kohl's surprise, Samuel was not one of them. She noticed, in fact, that he appeared distracted. As several of his classmates moved to the front of the room to play a role in *Huck Finn*, he stared down at his desk.

"How about you, Samuel?" Ms. Kohl asked. "Didn't you like the novel?"

"It was all right," he answered.

"Well everyone can't love every piece of literature and that's OK," she said, and continued with the lesson.

Johnny, one of Samuel's white classmates and closest friends, volunteered to play the role of Huck, which also made him the narrator of the story. He played his role with verve, trying his best to sound the way he imagined Huck sounding.

Initially Samuel sat quietly, following the story in his book. But within minutes Ms. Kohl noticed him growing listless, shifting in his seat.

"Everything OK, Samuel?" she asked.

"Not really," he answered.

"What's going on?"

"I hate this book."

"Yes, well, everyone can't love every piece of literature," Ms. Kohl said again. "Let's get through these first ten pages. Then I'd like to hear why you don't like it."

Samuel sighed.

Samuel's classmates continued to read. Ms. Kohl, noticing that Samuel remained uncomfortable, started to worry that it might be because of the racial language in the book.

And then they reached the eighth page of the novel. Ms. Kohl always felt a little nervous about page eight because although the n-word was scattered here and there through the first seven pages, it appears several times on page eight. Ms. Kohl's thoughts were interrupted by the sound of Samuel's shouting voice: "Stop it!" he screamed. "You think saying that is OK? Shut up!"

Samuel threw his book on the floor and left the room, slamming the door behind him. Ms. Kohl, looking up to find 26 students as shocked as she was, had no idea what to do next.

Questions

1 How might Ms. Kohl have prepared her students for the language in *Huckleberry Finn*? Should she have done so before they began reading the novel, or do you agree with her practice, in this case, of not wanting to "spoil" their experiences by talking too much about it before they read it?

2 Should teachers assign readings that use the n-word or other derogatory language with such a painful history? Some people argue that such language should be removed from literature used in schools. Do you agree? Why or why not?

3 Should Samuel be punished for his outburst and for walking out of the classroom the same way another student would have been if it had happened on another day for another reason? How might Ms. Kohl address the situation with her other students?

4 If you were Ms. Kohl, what strategies might you use to regain Samuel's trust and to rebuild a safe environment for him in your classroom?

Turn to page 140 to view the Points for Consideration for this case.

CASE 6.3: DIVERSE FRIENDS DAY

Mr. Carbondale had been a language arts teacher at West River High School, a suburban school about 15 miles outside a major city, for more than 20 years. When he started teaching there just out of college, the students, like the teachers and administrators, were almost all white. This had begun to change about ten years ago when gentrification and rising property taxes started driving more and more working-class families of color out of the city to seek affordable housing. Now more than 40 percent of the student body comprised students of color, most of whom were African American or Mexican American.

Unlike some of his colleagues, Mr. Carbondale was happy to see the racial demographics of West River's student body changing. In fact, during several faculty meetings over the past few years, he had raised the concern that, despite these shifts, the teachers and administrators remained virtually all white. "Diversity enriches all of us," he would say.

Mr. Carbondale often volunteered to represent his school at the weekend-long "Inclusive Excellence" conference hosted each year by his district. At the most recent of these conferences, he learned about several promising diversity resources and programs, but he found one program idea most intriguing: Diverse Friends Day. It was a program in which students were encouraged to spend one day interacting with classmates with whom they normally wouldn't interact. They would eat lunch at a new table, sit by different people during class, and challenge themselves to shake up their social groups in other ways. The goal of the program was to help students learn about the dangers and limitations of strictly defined social boundaries and to encourage greater intergroup interaction. When he returned from the conference, Mr. Carbondale was eager to share the idea with his colleagues.

The following Monday, Mr. Carbondale secured permission from Ms. Wright, his principal, to organize Diverse Friends Day for February 26, just one month away. He suggested, as well, that teachers and administrators should also participate, at least spending their lunch periods that day with colleagues with whom they normally wouldn't eat lunch.

Mr. Carbondale couldn't wait to share the news about the upcoming event with his fourth period junior language arts class. Having just read a series of Langston Hughes poems, they had spent the last several class periods in spirited discussions about race relations in the United States. He expected some resistance. These were high school students, after all, whose identities were influenced mostly by their social groups. But they were also curious about social groups to which they did not belong. Mr. Carbondale believed this curiosity would override their anxieties about stepping temporarily out of their comfort zones.

As he had guessed, when Mr. Carbondale told his class about Diverse Friends Day, a few students protested. However, several other students voiced support for the program. He noted, though, that Pam and Tariq, the two African American students in his class, and Julio, one of three Mexican American students in his class, remained silent during the conversation. Not wanting to put them on the spot, he decided to reach out to them after class to elicit their feedback.

Once class ended, Mr. Carbondale pulled Pam, Tariq, and Julio aside and asked them for their thoughts on Diverse Friends Day. "I know you mean well, Mr. Carbondale, but that program is racist," Pam told him.

Shocked, Mr. Carbondale asked her to elaborate.

"I don't know about 'racist'," Tariq interjected, "but I don't want to do it."

"I think it sounds kind of fun," Julio said, "but a lot of the people in this school don't like us. Some of them call us names. Why would we want to hang out with people who don't like us?" Mr. Carbondale nodded his head sympathetically.

"Why do you think it's racist?" Mr. Carbondale asked Pam, noticing the tension on her face.

"There's a lot of racism in this school. Lunch is the only time I can relax, when I'm not feeling judged. I think Diverse Friends Day is for white people."

Unsettled and not sure what to say next, Mr. Carbondale thanked the students for their candor. As they left he added, "I'll think about what you shared and reconsider the idea."

Questions

1 Why might Pam have interpreted this program as "racist"? What did she mean when she said, "I think Diverse Friends Day is for white people"?

2 How might West River High School address the racial inequities being experienced by these students while also organizing programs meant to celebrate diversity? How might these approaches address the institutional culture of the school rather than just a problem of race relations among individual students?

3 Pam told Mr. Carbondale that lunch is the only time during school when she can relax without feeling judged by white students. Other than students of color at a predominantly white school, what sorts of students might share that experience with Pam?

4 Can you think of other "diversity" programs in schools that might elicit similar reactions from some students of color? What sort of program do you think Pam, Tariq, and Julio would support based on their reaction to Diverse Friends Day?

Turn to page 141 to view the Points for Consideration for this case.

CASE 6.4: TERMS OF ENDEARMENT

Ms. Lawson was glad to be teaching math at Greenstown High School, a racially and economically diverse school. She previously had worked at predominantly white schools with very few students receiving free or reduced-price lunch. After losing her job due to budget cuts, and after taking a course on diversity while earning her Masters of Arts in Teaching degree, she accepted a job teaching in a more diverse environment. She arrived at Greenstown feeling eager and prepared to take instructional advantage of the diversity.

Several weeks into her first year at Greenstown, Ms. Lawson was happy about how well she had adjusted to her new environment. She had taken several measures early in the school year to demonstrate her commitment to racial equity and it seemed as though students were responding positively. She was especially pleased when she saw students of color reading the Diversity in Mathematics posters she hung around the room, highlighting historically important mathematicians of color from around the world. They complained a little— predictably, she thought—in all of her classes on the second day of school when, responding to the racially segregated seating patterns she noticed the first day of class, she assigned seats. She never mentioned her reason for assigning seats, though, and students were accustomed to seat assignments from some of their other classes, so that tension passed quickly. All in all, things were progressing smoothly.

One afternoon around mid-October, as she gathered her materials for her fifth period class and students made their way into her classroom, Ms. Lawson overhead one of her students use the n-word. Understanding how inflammatory the n-word was, her immediate reaction was concern that there would be a fight in her classroom. So when she looked up from her desk and peered toward the back of her classroom, where she was sure the word came from, she was surprised to see Reggie, an African American student, Adolfo, a Latino student, and Anthony, a white student, all laughing together.

"Who said that?" Ms. Lawson asked as she stood and walked toward the back of the room.

"Said what?" Adolfo asked, still laughing.

"You all know exactly what I mean. The n-word," Ms. Lawson replied. Nobody responded, but Adolfo and Reggie both glanced at Anthony.

"Anthony?" Ms. Lawson prodded.

"I didn't say the n-word, I said *n-i-g-g-a, nigga,*" he explained. Ms. Lawson was unsettled by how confident Anthony sounded, as though he really did not believe he had done anything wrong. "I always call Reggie that. He's cool with it. It's a term of endearment."

Keisha, an African American young woman who had overheard their conversation, interjected. "That's not a term of endearment, you idiot. It's racist. And you're lucky you're not getting a beat down right now for saying it."

"Enough of that," Ms. Lawson said, glaring at Keisha. "There won't be any threats of violence in this classroom. Sit down and let me take care of this."

Unsure what to say next, Ms. Lawson turned toward Reggie. He was no longer laughing and, she thought, was beginning to look uncomfortable. "Is that true, Reggie, that he calls you that all the time and you're fine with it?"

"It's no big deal," Anthony explained. "Right, Reg?" he asked playfully, nudging Reggie with his elbow.

"Reggie can speak for himself," Ms. Lawson said, then looked back at Reggie, who was looking even more uncomfortable. Just then, the start of class bell rang and Ms. Lawson looked up to see everybody in the room staring at her and Reggie. Feeling that whatever he really felt about Anthony's use of the n-word, Reggie was even more uneasy with the spotlight she was shining on him in that moment, she decided to drop the issue and commence to teaching class.

As she walked back toward her desk, she said with a half-defeated sigh, "Please remember, everyone, that one of our community norms is *respect*. I don't care you how pronounce it or what you mean by it, there is no room in this classroom for that kind of language."

She knew, even as she was making that statement, that she did not handle the situation well. She also knew she needed to figure out a way to respond more thoughtfully in case it happened again.

Questions

1 Did Anthony's explanation about how he wasn't really using the n-word make his actions less of a problem? Is there any circumstance in which it would be acceptable for somebody to use the n-word or any variation of it in a classroom or school? If so, what would that circumstance be?

2 When Keisha voiced her displeasure about Anthony's language, Ms. Lawson, worried that the tension would escalate, chastised her and ordered her to sit down. How could she have addressed Keisha's comments more effectively?

3 Ms. Lawson put Reggie on the spot by asking him how he felt about the situation in front of his friends, in front of Keisha, and in front of whomever else was in earshot as students filed into the room. What are some other ways Ms. Lawson might have checked in with Reggie in order to avoid shining the spotlight on him in that way?

4 Ms. Lawson knew she needed to address the use of the n-word with her entire class, as she couldn't be sure how many students overheard the conversation. How might you approach such a task?

Turn to page 142 to view the Points for Consideration for this case.

CASE 6.5: AN UNCOMFORTABLE FIELD TRIP

It was field trip day and Ms. Anderson, a teacher at Meadow Brook High School, was excited. She had sent a letter asking for a representative of a renowned advertising agency to visit one of her classes during a marketing unit and was pleasantly surprised when the agency responded with the suggestion that, instead of an employee coming to the school, the class should visit the agency for a private tour. The day would be filled with opportunities for students to learn about careers in marketing. They would even be treated to a catered lunch. Ms. Anderson hoped the trip would be inspirational to her students, many of whom soon would be first-generation college students and had limited exposure to the business world.

The day before the field trip, Ms. Anderson reminded the students to dress more formally than they usually dressed for school. However, as she watched the students trickle into class on field trip day, she noticed that two of her students of color, Alejandro and Kevin, were wearing sneakers with their dress pants. Not wanting to embarrass them, she walked over to them and jokingly said, "Sneakers? I guess you two will be ready if we play basketball during the visit." Both boys laughed as they sat down, then listened to Ms. Anderson discuss behavior expectations for the day.

Later, when the students arrived at the ad agency, a company representative greeted them and proceeded to lead them on a tour. As they walked through one of the main workspaces, the tour leader mentioned that many of the employees were hired directly out of college and that many of them had attended the finest colleges in the country. "If you have excellent grades and work hard, you could end up working here," she said, then added, "and once you're in we take good care of you."

Ms. Anderson noticed that Alejandro and Kevin looked at each other and rolled their eyes in response to the tour guide's comment. Then she saw Kevin whisper something to Alejandro, at which they both laughed quietly. Ms. Anderson approached them discreetly, reminding them to be respectful.

As the tour continued, she saw Alejandro smirk in response to a comment made by one of the agency executives to whom the class was introduced. Feeling frustrated and a little embarrassed, Ms. Anderson pulled him aside and told him how generous the ad agency was to invite the students on this tour. "We should be appreciative, not disrespectful," she chided. "If this continues," she added, "you'll have to wait in the lobby with me and miss the rest of the day's activities." Alejandro and Kevin remained quiet for the remainder of the field trip, but appeared disengaged and annoyed that their teacher had drawn attention to their behavior.

Once they had returned to the school, Ms. Anderson asked the class to share what impressed them most about the trip. A few students mentioned how fun it was to be downtown and to visit such an impressive workplace. Others talked about still feeling hungry after their "fancy lunch."

When Ms. Anderson asked whether they would want to work at the agency, a few students nodded. Kevin responded with a grin, "It seems like *you* want to work there, Ms. A." Several students laughed. Kevin continued, "It was good not having to be at school, though."

Really? Ms. Anderson thought to herself once the students left. *I guess I took the wrong group of students.* She wondered what she could have done differently to make the day more of a success.

Questions

1 Why might Kevin and Alejandro have been wearing sneakers with their dress pants? Was Ms. Anderson's comment to them about being ready to play basketball an appropriate attempt to connect with them? How would you have handled the situation differently, if at all?

2 Why might some of Ms. Anderson's students have been uncomfortable at the ad agency? What might have kept some of them from just letting Ms. Anderson know they were uncomfortable? How might she have given the boys a chance during the trip to express their reactions?

3 In what ways, if at all, should Ms. Anderson have prepared her students for this field trip? In what ways could she have prepared the ad agency to mindfully host her students?

4 What do you think Ms. Anderson meant by "the wrong group of students"?

Turn to page 142 to view the Points for Consideration for this case.

7

Cases on Sex, Gender, and Gender Identity

CASE 7.1: BOYS VERSUS GIRLS TRIVIA CONTEST

Mr. Matthews, a first-year teacher, walked into his mentor Mr. Williams's classroom, excited to observe him teaching his fourth-period geography class. Mr. Matthews had a lot of respect for Mr. Williams as a teacher and was looking forward to seeing effective classroom management techniques in action. Mr. Williams, a 15-year teaching veteran, was well liked by students and his colleagues. Their principal had recommended that Mr. Matthews observe Mr. Williams for an hour, homing in on how he engaged students and fostered high levels of classroom participation, the keys to limiting disciplinary interruptions. As the students filed in, Mr. Matthews found a desk in the back of the room and prepared to take notes.

As his students settled into their seats, Mr. Williams called out cheerily, "Good afternoon, boys and girls! Are we ready to learn?"

"We are ready!" the students responded in unison, clearly knowing it was part of their daily routine.

Mr. Williams smiled at Mr. Matthews and whispered, "That's how we begin every class. They know to start paying attention."

Turning back to his students, Mr. Williams reminded them that one of their benchmark tests was scheduled for the next day. Following a brief overview of strategies for studying the material in their texts, Mr. Williams asked the students whether they wanted to play a game. "Let's see how prepared you are for the exam." The students agreed eagerly.

"First, we need to split ourselves into two teams," Mr. Williams explained before asking the class how they wanted to divide themselves. As the students discussed options, Mr. Williams walked to the back of the room and said to Mr. Matthews, "If you let students make decisions, they'll take ownership of their learning."

Several students suggested that they form teams by gender, "boys versus girls," eliciting enthusiastic support from many of their classmates. Mr. Williams sent the young men to one side of the room and the young women to the other side of room, and then proceeded to ask each team questions while keeping count of correct responses.

After ten minutes the "girls" team was well ahead of the "boys" team, leading a couple of young men to joke that they were "letting the girls win so that they won't cry." A couple of young women responded by reminding their male classmates that the "girls" won the previous two games as well. Following several minutes of the teams mocking each other, Mr. Williams attempted to refocus the class by jokingly saying, "All right guys, listen up. If you don't stop fighting I'm going to prepare a new seating chart, and it will alternate boys and girls, which clearly would make you all unhappy. Let's focus!" Both teams refocused on the game.

After class, as students left the room, Mr. Matthews heard several of them, young women and young men, laughing and making disparaging remarks to each other, debating about which gender was most intelligent. Mr. Williams approached Mr. Matthews and warmly said, "That's how it's done. The students love competitions and don't even realize how much they're learning in the process. Any behavior issues are resolved quickly when I threaten to give them assigned seats. They hate that."

He then looked down and, seeing Mr. Matthews's notes, noticed that he had written and circled "gender stereotypes" in his notebook. "Whoa! *That's* what you are focusing on?" Mr. Williams asked, sounding offended. "Boys versus girls: that's what the students love to do. It's a fun way to help them learn." He then counseled Mr. Matthews, "You're still new at this and will learn soon enough that as long as the students are engaged and learning, that other stuff doesn't matter."

With that, Mr. Williams walked back to his desk as Mr. Matthews sat speechless, wondering whether he had been too sensitive.

Questions

1 What are some of the dynamics Mr. Matthews observed that might have raised concerns about gender stereotypes for him?

2 Is Mr. Matthews's assessment of "gender stereotypes" justified? Why or why not?

3 What implications about gender might arise for the students in this class? How might students who are transgender or who do not identify with any particular gender group feel as they watch their peers enthusiastically endorse the "boys versus girls" activity?

4 What are some other options for splitting students into two teams?

Turn to page 143 to view the Points for Consideration for this case.

CASE 7.2: GENDER BIAS WITH A SMILE

Ms. Braxton, a science teacher in her third year at Seneca Bluff Middle School, was passionate about encouraging young women to imagine themselves as future scientists. This is what inspired her to become a teacher after spending 15 years in the corporate world, where she tested the safety of cosmetics products for several companies. The pay cut was severe when she took the job at the school, but her job satisfaction was much, much higher.

As a woman with a graduate degree in biochemistry, Ms. Braxton still carried with her the negative memories of feeling invisible in advanced science courses, where some of her high school teachers and college professors seemed to favor male students, who were always in the majority. She often felt like she did not belong, though she did well in her classes. As she advanced through upper-level science courses in high school, then through a Bachelor of Science and a Master of Science program in college, she saw fewer and fewer women, whether classmates or faculty members. Nobody ever *told her* she didn't belong, but she did occasionally overhear jokes from her classmates or professors about women's inferiority in the sciences.

This is why, although she encouraged all of her students to see themselves not just as science students, but as *scientists*, she was especially conscious of encouraging young women to pursue their science interests. She was sure to hang as many photographs of female scientists around the room as she did male scientists and never failed to mention when women made important discoveries or breakthroughs related to something the students were studying.

Ms. Braxton decided that this year she was going to acknowledge Women's History Month by setting aside one day in all of her classes to talk about prominent, modern women scientists and ways in which they were helping to create a better world. After she mentioned the idea in a faculty meeting, Mr. Cameron, the school's assistant principal, asked if he could observe one of her classes that day.

"This is just the sort of thing we ought to be doing," he said, surprising Ms. Braxton, who worried she would be discouraged from spending a full day on something that never would be measured on a standardized test.

"You're welcome any time," Ms. Braxton replied.

A few weeks later, when Mr. Cameron entered Ms. Braxton's eighth grade science class for the observation, he was pleased to see how engaged the students were. Ms. Braxton had created a slideshow highlighting the careers of five scientists who were women. What the students seemed most interested in, though, were her practical descriptions of how their work was related to the daily lives of the students themselves. Ms. Braxton was thrilled that so many of the young women in her class were asking questions.

Suddenly Tricia, one of Ms. Braxton's students, turned to Mr. Cameron. "Hey, Mr. C.," she asked, "why didn't we learn about this stuff in sixth or seventh grade science?"

"Yeah," Shelley agreed. "I never heard of any of these people."

Mr. Cameron, always affable, smiled. "Ms. Braxton, as a female scientist, herself, has a special interest in this area," he explained, "and it's wonderful that she's passing that on to you girls."

Ms. Braxton appreciated Mr. Cameron's comment, but she also felt that it was important for the young men in the room, not just the young women, to learn about women scientists, their contributions to the world, and the challenges they faced. However, she liked the fact that her students were raising these questions with the assistant principal, so she figured she could make that point later in the period.

"But why aren't they even in our textbooks?" Tricia asked, still looking at Mr. Cameron. "It's almost all men."

"Well," Ms. Braxton began to respond, before Mr. Cameron cut her off.

"You have to remember," he explained in his usual friendly tone, "that until recently, many women just weren't interested in science. Plus, the women you're learning about today are unique because women's brains are not wired for science or math the way men's brains are. That's what makes Ms. Braxton so special and why you're lucky to have her as a teacher."

Ms. Braxton scrambled to find a way to respond to Mr. Cameron that would make it clear she did not agree with him while avoiding starting an argument with him in front of the students. She felt that, in some ways, he had just undone a lot of what she did throughout the semester, especially with the young women in her class, but she also realized that Mr. Cameron, universally adored by the students, meant no harm. What, she wondered, should she do?

Questions

1 Ms. Braxton purposefully included contributions of women scientists throughout the school year, so why was it important for her students also to learn about women scientists on a designated day?

2 Ms. Braxton believed that learning about women's contributions in science was as important for the young men in her class as it was for the young women. Do you agree? Why or why not?

3 Mr. Cameron believed he was complimenting Ms. Braxton when he pointed out how exceptional she was as a woman scientist. Why did Ms. Braxton not hear his comment as a compliment?

4 Should Ms. Braxton respond to Mr. Cameron in the moment, with the students in the room? How might she present a different view if she were to respond right away? Given Mr. Cameron's status as the assistant principal, how might Ms. Braxton help students to think critically about his comments if she were to wait until he no longer was in the room?

5 If you were in Ms. Braxton's shoes, how might you address this issue with Mr. Cameron when you have a moment with him in private?

Turn to page 144 to view the Points for Consideration for this case.

CASE 7.3: TIMMY'S GENDER NONCONFORMITY

Timmy, a student in Ms. Grover's third grade class at Sully Elementary School, was often teased by classmates because he displayed what they interpreted to be "girl" qualities. Ms. Grover had been warned of this situation by Mr. Franks and Ms. Puterio, Timmy's kindergarten and second grade teachers. In fact, ever since his kindergarten year at the school, teachers and administrators had noticed not only that Timmy preferred to play with girls and was noticeably uncomfortable interacting with boys, but that he much preferred stereotypically "girl" toys and books.

Mr. Franks noted that, as a kindergartner, Timmy gravitated toward the play station that contained a chest full of costumes. He especially liked a princess gown and tiara that were kept in the chest. At that time the children didn't seem to care much. They made an occasional remark about *those being girls' clothes* or *toys* or *books*, but Mr. Franks always stepped in quickly to say that all of the clothes and toys and books in the room were for everybody. He was a little worried that Timmy's parents might not approve of this approach, but his mother, who always picked him up from school and often saw him playing with girls or carrying around a doll, never said a word about it.

Timmy's first and second grade teachers handled the situation similarly, but noticed that the teasing was slowly intensifying. Ms. Puterio noticed the same thing and, like Mr. Franks, was always quick to defend Timmy. She also saw, to her disappointment, that several of the girls who had been friendly with Timmy began to nudge him out of their social circles and join in on the teasing. She tried to speak with the girls about this, urging them to be nice to Timmy, but it didn't help. Timmy, who was not very outspoken anyway, did not seem very upset about losing friends, and nothing had escalated into a physical altercation, so Ms. Puterio did not worry too much about it. She knew, though, that as Timmy grew older the teasing would become fiercer and somebody would need to intervene in a more serious way.

One day, a few months into the school year, Ms. Grover noticed that several students were standing around Timmy's desk, pointing and laughing. "What's going on back there?" she inquired.

"Timmy's a girl!" one of the students shouted, eliciting attention and laughter from around the classroom.

"He painted his fingernails, like a girl," another student said, giggling.

"It's just *one* nail," Timmy muttered softly, bending forward and hiding his face in his arms, which were crossed on the desk in front of him.

Approaching Timmy's desk, Ms. Grover could see that the pinky nail on his left hand was painted white. "Everybody take your seats. There will be no teasing in this classroom. We are who we are and we respect one another."

As the students were taking their seats Ms. Grover kneeled down next to Timmy's desk and asked, in a whisper, "Do your parents know you painted your fingernail?"

"My mom knows," he whispered back, tears in his eyes. "She only would let me paint one."

Ms. Grover felt conflicted. On the one hand, she knew children could be brutal with each other over gender identity and that a majority of bullying at school happens beyond the earshot of teachers. She did not quite understand what was going on with Timmy, but she wanted him to be able to express himself in whatever way felt right for him. She also knew, though, that she and the other teachers could not protect Timmy from the increasingly harsh bullying he was going to have to endure, especially down the road when he would start middle school.

Part of her wanted to urge Timmy's parents to convince him to try to fit in a little better at school—to refuse to allow him to come to school with nail polish, to make him cut his hair a little shorter, and maybe even to help him try to make friends with some of the boys in his class. Another part of her wanted to figure out a way to create a safe environment for Timmy exactly as Timmy wanted to be, but she knew that would take a school-wide team effort on the part of every adult in the building, and she was not sure everybody would be on board. She also figured she needed to find some educational way to address what was going on with her students despite not fully understanding it herself, and to do so without further alienating Timmy.

Questions

1 Timmy's teachers from kindergarten through second grade, despite noticing that he was being teased more and more, chose not to intervene, except for quashing the teasing. Should they have done something more, such as educating students about gender identity? If so, in your opinion, at what age would addressing gender identity issues be appropriate?

2 How should Ms. Grover broach this conversation with Timmy's parents? Timmy specified that his *mom* knew he had painted his fingernail. Should Ms. Grover reach out to Timmy's mother, specifically, unsure about whether his father knew about the situation?

3 How would you, if you were Timmy's teacher, have responded to the teasing Timothy was experiencing? How would you have reached out to Timmy, mindful not to draw unwanted attention to him?

4 Part of Ms. Grover's challenge is that although she wanted to try to make the school a more welcoming place for Timmy, she was unsure of her ability to do so. This led her to wonder whether it might be safer for Timmy to conform while he is at school. What would you advise Ms. Grover to do?

Turn to page 145 to view the Points for Consideration for this case.

CASE 7.4: INTERNET OBJECTIFICATION

Petra, an eighth grader at Shirley Chisholm Middle School, was usually full of energy and smiles. So Ms. Alexandra was a little surprised on Monday morning before first period when Petra walked into her classroom looking sullen and pale.

"Are you feeling OK?" Ms. Alexandra asked as Petra headed sluggishly toward her desk.

"Yeah," Petra answered feebly, avoiding eye contact.

A few minutes later Ms. Alexandra noticed a few of her male students looking at Petra and smirking. One of the students, Tyler, was holding his phone up so other students could see it. "Brutal," Tiffany said, pointing at the phone.

Ms. Alexandra, sensing a connection between Petra's discomfort and whatever Tyler, Tiffany, and their friends were seeing on the screen, approached the group. Tyler quickly turned off his phone and slipped it into his pocket.

"What's going on here, Tyler?" Ms. Alexandra asked.

"Nothing," he replied. "I was just showing them a Facebook page on my phone."

Ms. Alexandra reminded Tyler that he was only allowed to use his phone during class to look up information relevant to schoolwork. "If I see you on Facebook again," she warned, "I'll have to take that phone until the end of the day."

She then looked back over at Petra, whose head was buried in her arms. Concerned, Ms. Alexandra approached Petra, tapped her on the shoulder, and motioned her toward the hallway. Petra stood up slowly and followed Ms. Alexandra.

"What in the world is going on, Petra?" Ms. Alexandra asked, touching her softly on the arm. "I can see that you're upset and I want to help, but I can't help if I don't know what's going on." Petra shook her head. "Is it something on Facebook?" Ms. Alexandra prodded to no avail. Petra started crying.

At that moment Ms. Santos, Chisholm's assistant principal, turned the corner. She was walking toward Ms. Alexandra and Petra in a hurry, carrying her tablet computer.

"Are you OK?" Ms. Santos asked Petra, handing Ms. Alexandra her tablet. A Facebook page entitled "Chisholm Chicks" was on the screen. At the top of the page was a photo of Petra in a swimsuit— what looked like a swim team photo. Beneath the photo were a series of numbers between one and ten and brief comments about Petra's attractiveness, such as "was hotter last year," "could use a makeover" and "she's ok, nothing special." Ms. Alexandra recognized the names of some, but not all, of the young men who had left comments.

"Oh no," Ms. Alexandra said, giving Petra a hug.

"I guess that means you hadn't seen this before?" Ms. Santos asked. Before Ms. Alexandra could answer, Ms. Santos explained, "The author of this page is in your class, too, which is one of the reasons I hurried down here."

"Tyler?" Ms. Alexandra inquired, nodding. "He was showing this to other students. Even some of the girls in class were laughing at it."

Ms. Santos responded, "This is something he started on Friday. It's been a different girl every day since then. A couple of students' parents called to give me a heads-up."

"Well, I'm going to put an end to this right now," Ms. Alexandra exclaimed as she stepped back toward her classroom door.

"No, wait!" Petra pleaded, grabbing her teacher's arm. This startled Ms. Alexandra, who had almost forgotten that Petra was standing there because she had been so quiet. Petra continued, "Please don't say anything. That'll make it worse. Please!"

"OK," Ms. Santos said reassuringly. "Well, for now why don't you take your seat and let Ms. Alexandra and I chat." Ms. Alexandra and Ms. Santos could hear some laughter as Petra walked back into the room, making them both cringe and reminding them that they had just sent her into a hostile environment.

Ms. Alexandra asked whether this situation was covered under the school's anti-bullying policy.

"Absolutely," Ms. Santos replied, "or at least it should be. My bigger concern is how we can hold Tyler accountable and address this issue with the students without making Petra and the other girls on that Facebook page even bigger targets."

Ms. Alexandra sighed and nodded.

"For now," Ms. Santos continued, "I'm going to take Tyler with me to the office. Go ahead and start your lesson for today and we'll reconnect at lunch time."

"OK," Ms. Alexandra said before taking a deep breath and heading back into her classroom.

Questions

1 Petra asked Ms. Alexandra and Ms. Santos not to do anything to address the incident for fear that it would escalate the bullying

and harassment she was experiencing. How would you have responded in that situation if you were Ms. Alexandra or Ms. Santos?

2 Is Ms. Santos doing the right thing by taking Tyler to the office with her? Why or why not?

3 Ms. Alexandra was surprised that girls in her class would participate in teasing Petra about the photo and comments. What are some reasons why young women might participate in this sort of thing?

4 What are some of the ways in which you have seen social media used to facilitate bullying, sexual harassment, or other types of bias and discrimination? What role should schools play in addressing social media harassment, bias, and discrimination?

Turn to page 146 to view the Points for Consideration for this case.

8

CASES ON (DIS)ABILITY

CASE 8.1: A "SURPRISE" FIRE DRILL

Ms. Stintson, a special education teacher at Centennial Elementary School, enjoyed working with her colleagues and helping them to understand the unique needs of her students. Her colleagues always seemed open to her ideas and appreciative of her work. Recently, though, she sensed a little frustration on the part of Ms. Foster, a first grade teacher, who recently received a new student with an Individualized Education Plan (IEP) in her class. The student, a boy named Aiden, previously attended school in another state and brought his IEP, which addressed how best to meet his learning needs, with him to Centennial.

Aiden had been diagnosed with an Autism Spectrum Disorder but functioned well in a mainstream classroom. Ms. Foster seemed to think that many of the IEP objectives were unnecessary because Aiden was progressing just as well as his peers. She often expressed this sentiment with Ms. Stintson. Ms. Stintson, in turn, reminded her that she needed to continue adhering to the plan, but also mentioned that classroom teachers have an opportunity to share concerns during the upcoming annual review.

One Friday, before the school day began, the principal pulled Ms. Stintson aside and informed her that he would be administering a surprise fire drill later that morning. He asked her to take necessary measures to ensure that her students would not be negatively affected by the event.

One of the students Ms. Stintson immediately thought about was Aiden, whose parents had indicated that loud noises scared him so much they could disrupt his entire week. Although this concern was not yet indicated in his IEP, Aiden's parents had asked Ms. Stintson if she could notify Aiden about fire drills before they occurred and provide him with noise-reducing headphones.

Ms. Stintson stopped by Ms. Foster's classroom to share the plan with her. "I'll sneak in a minute or so before the alarm goes off to give Aiden the headphones," Ms. Stintson explained. "Then I will escort him out of the school with the rest of the class."

Ms. Foster expressed concerns about this arrangement. "It isn't a *surprise* fire drill if the students see you preparing Aiden for it," she complained. "These students are young. They're still learning the procedures to follow if there is a fire. The best thing we can do for *all* of them is to make the drill as authentic as possible." After a short pause, she continued: "Plus, if it's not mandated in Aiden's IEP, I don't think we should do it. You wouldn't be able to come in and give him headphones if it were a *real* fire."

Ms. Stintson had anticipated Ms. Foster's resistance and reminded her of the parents' request. She mentioned the potentially severe consequences for Aiden if he were taken by surprise and subjected unexpectedly to the noise and chaos of a fire drill. "I understand your desire to make it authentic," she explained, "but we can't knowingly subject Aiden to a harmful experience."

"I promise that I'll be discreet," Ms. Stintson continued. "It *is* in Aiden's best interest to remain with his classmates so he will be prepared if there is a real fire."

"Sorry," Ms. Foster responded curtly. "If you think headphones are necessary, then you'll need to take him out of my classroom well in advance of the drill so the other students don't suspect anything. That's my best compromise. I need to keep all my students' safety in mind."

Ms. Foster left the room before Ms. Stintson could respond.

Ms. Stintson sighed and glanced at the headphones she had carried into Ms. Foster's classroom. Her initial impulse was to notify the principal or Aiden's parents about Ms. Foster's unwillingness to help, but she worried about how that might affect Ms. Foster's relationship with Aiden. She certainly did not want Ms. Foster to resent having Aiden in her class. However, she did want to find a constructive way to advocate for Aiden.

Questions

1 Do you agree with Ms. Stintson, who is concerned primarily about how a fire drill might traumatize Aiden, or with Ms. Foster, who worries that the accommodation will make the experience less authentic to him and the other students? Why? To what extent do the wishes of Aiden's parents inform your opinion?

2 What might you have recommended to Ms. Stintson and Ms. Foster as an alternative compromise, or is a compromise not an option in this case?

3 What options does Ms. Stintson have for advocating for Aiden in this situation? How would you advocate for him?

Turn to page 146 to view the Points for Consideration for this case.

CASE 8.2: INSUFFICIENT ACCOMMODATIONS

Ms. Thurston, a sixth grade science teacher, always believed in the power of experiential learning. Students didn't learn science by studying concepts out of a book, she thought, but by being scientists, using their senses and their reasoning skills to explore and apply scientific concepts.

One of Ms. Thurston's favorite activities, and one she arranged every year, involved taking her students to Meadow Creek Park, a nearby nature reserve, where they could walk the same trails and explore the same terrain as scientists from the university who studied local ecology. She was especially excited this year because the park had hired a new education director, Ms. Parsons, who had designed a 1-mile conservation hike specifically for middle school students, basing much of its content on sixth, seventh, and eighth grade state science standards. Ms. Thurston couldn't wait to take her students on that hike!

Two weeks before the field trip to Meadow Creek Park, a new student, Justin, was added to Ms. Thurston's fourth-period science class. A cheery young man who was especially enthusiastic about science, Justin had cerebral palsy, a condition that required him to use crutches. At first Ms. Thurston was concerned about whether or not Justin would be able to participate in the field trip. He could navigate the classroom and school pretty easily. But because she never had *needed* to know, Ms. Thurston was not sure whether the learning center in the park was accessible. Certainly it met basic Americans with Disabilities Act standards with ramps, accessible parking, and wheelchair accessible bathrooms, but these were minimal standards.

Ms. Thurston decided to call Ms. Parsons and inquire about the accommodations offered for students like Justin. The last thing she wanted to do was to discourage his love of science with a negative experience, especially considering his newness at the school. Ms. Parsons tried to assure her by saying, "The hike might be a bit much for Justin, but we have alternative opportunities for students with physical disabilities and learning differences. He'll be fine."

When the bus pulled up to the Meadow Creek learning center, where the students were to check in and hear a short talk about being safe and respecting nature in the reserve, Ms. Parsons was there to greet them. Ms. Thurston was thrilled to see the expanded gardens wrapping around the south side of the building and the fairly smooth paths webbing through them. Perhaps Justin would be able to do some nature exploring after all, she thought.

As the students listened to their short lesson and asked their tour guides questions, Ms. Thurston talked with Ms. Parsons about how they would accommodate Justin. "Looks like he can spend some time in the garden," Ms. Thurston said, "exploring some of the region's native plants and flowers."

"Unfortunately," Ms. Parsons responded, "park rules don't allow for that." She pointed to a sign hanging above the door leading through the gardens and around to the hiking trails. It was labeled "General Rules of the Reserve." The third rule read: "For their own safety, visitors with conditions, injuries, or illnesses which may impair their mobility are not permitted on the nature paths or in the gardens. A selection of films about the park and local ecology are available for people who are unable to participate in the hikes due to these conditions."

Shocked, Ms. Thurston replied, "I thought you said you had accommodations. A film isn't an accommodation!"

Heading back toward the students, who were gathered at the south side exit, Ms. Thurston felt unsure. Should she use this as a teachable moment? What should she say to Justin, and how could she still make this a meaningful learning experience for him?

"The travails of experiential learning," she thought, wondering what to do next.

Questions

1 Ms. Thurston was frustrated to find that the learning "accommodation" for Justin consisted of sitting *inside* the center and watching a film while his classmates were on the hike. In your estimation, does this constitute an equitable accommodation? If not, what sorts of accommodations might have been more equitable?

2 Is it Ms. Thurston's responsibility to provide the hike experience to most of her students even if one student is excluded from any sort of parallel learning opportunity at the park? Should she look for a different learning opportunity that could include all of her students, even if she feels that opportunity may not generate the same level of enthusiasm for most of her student as hiking in Meadow Creek Park?

3 How, as she approaches her students after talking with Ms. Parsons, might Ms. Thurston use this situation as a teachable moment for *all* of her students? Can she do so without risking making Justin uncomfortable?

4 Now that the class is at the park, prepared to begin the hike while Justin watches a film, how might Ms. Thurston make the best of what she interprets as an inequitable situation?

Turn to page 147 to view the Points for Consideration for this case.

CASE 8.3: NUT ALLERGY

Katelyn, a second grader at Beachwood Elementary School, had a nut allergy that required extra precautions to ensure her safety while at school.

Katelyn's teacher, Mr. Hughes, was a veteran educator who willingly made accommodations in his class so that Katelyn never felt like she was missing out due to her allergy. Some of these accommodations included having all students wash their hands diligently before returning from lunch and making sure that they did not bring snacks from home into the classroom. He clearly communicated his "nut-free" policy to all of his students' families during the back-to-school meeting. He also sought training from the school nurse on how to use an epinephrine auto-injector, so that, if necessary, he could administer medication to Katelyn in order to prevent anaphylactic shock.

Mr. Hughes even included lessons and activities throughout the school year about the uniqueness of every child and how they can all learn from one another. He prided himself on being proactive rather than reactive when it came to meeting his students' needs.

At the beginning of the school year, Katelyn's mother, Ms. Thomas, asked Mr. Hughes if she could chaperone all of the class's field trips so she would be present if Katelyn experienced an allergic reaction. Mr. Hughes agreed, but also mentioned that parents and guardians typically attend only one field trip during the year so that other parents would have an opportunity to chaperone a trip as well. He forewarned her that other parents and guardians might complain about her chaperoning every trip, but said he would do his best to support her.

"Katelyn's safety is more important than people's misperceptions and resentments," Ms. Thomas, who was used to encountering resistance from people at the school, replied. Mr. Hughes appreciated her advocacy for her daughter.

When Mr. Hughes sent permission slips for field trips and requests for adult chaperones home, he was mindful to reduce the number of chaperones he needed by one in order to reserve a spot for Ms. Thomas. He received occasional complaints from parents and guardians about Ms. Thomas being permitted to attend each trip—certainly fewer than he had anticipated. He was always quick to point out how helpful it was to have Ms. Thomas on the trips so he could focus on the rest of the class.

Then he sent home permission slips and chaperone requests for the last field trip of the year: a visit to their state's capitol building. For several weeks the students had been learning about the state government. They were excited to see their elected officials in action. The day he sent the permission slips home, Mr. Hughes learned that his class had been invited to watch their governor deliver a live press conference. They would even have time to ask her questions and take photos with her. Mr. Hughes and his students were thrilled.

Unfortunately, due to space and security restrictions imposed by the governor's office, only a handful of parents could chaperone. That evening, Mr. Hughes received several emails from interested parents and guardians asking if they could join the class on the field trip. Many expressed their desire to share the exciting moment with their children. Several mentioned how they ought to be allowed to join this field trip because they hadn't attended any of the others. Regretfully, Mr. Hughes had to deny most of the requests. He did promise, though, to take plenty of photographs and videos if he was allowed to do so.

The next day, as he was taking morning attendance, he noticed Katelyn looking unusually sad. "What's wrong, Katelyn?" he asked.

Katelyn responded that her classmates were being mean to her about their moms or dads not being allowed to attend the trip "because my mom *has to come*." Through a sniffle she continued, "They say it's not fair since she came on the other trips."

"It's just an excuse," Jennie, one of Katelyn's classmates, said. "We've never even seen you get sick from nuts."

Mr. Hughes was shocked, and decided to address this issue with the whole class. This prompted candid responses from his students, many of whom said their parents had been complaining at home.

Nathan shared, "My mom said she was going to talk to the principal about how you save spots for some parents and that's not fair."

Mr. Hughes glanced at Katelyn, who now had tears streaming down her face. *I'm not going to change my policy*, thought Mr. Hughes, *but I definitely need to do* something *differently*.

Questions

1 Were Mr. Hughes's accommodations for Katelyn, such as allowing her mother to chaperone every field trip, necessary or just considerate?

2 Mr. Hughes did not want to change his policy but did want to do
   a better job addressing the concerns shared by Katelyn's classmates and their parents and guardians. If he came to you for
   advice on what he might do differently, what would you suggest?
3 What policies exist in your class, school, or district, or in other
   districts, pertaining to nut allergies or other similar medical
   conditions? In your opinion, are these policies adequate? If not,
   what else could schools do to ensure the safety of students who
   are diagnosed with a food allergy?
4 Mr. Hughes was committed to maintaining an equitable and
   inclusive environment in his classroom. Given his students'
   comments about Katelyn and the fact that they might have been
   hearing negative things about Katelyn and her mother at home,
   how should he have addressed this situation with his students?

Turn to page 148 to view the Points for Consideration for this case.

9

CASES ON SEXUAL ORIENTATION

CASE 9.1: A NEW CLUB

Ms. Green, a history and civics teacher at Halloway High School, was a strong proponent of student efficacy. She only needed to utter the first half of her hallmark phrase, "If it's change you want . . .," before her students finished it for her: ". . . then it's change you must create." Many students who felt alienated or disconnected at Halloway gravitated toward Ms. Green and her classroom.

It was little surprise, then, when Lorraine, one of two "out" lesbian, gay, bisexual, or queer-identifying (LGBQ) students at the school, asked Ms. Green if she would be willing to serve as the faculty sponsor for a Gay–Straight Alliance, or "GSA," a student organization for LGBQ students and their allies. Lorraine explained to Ms. Green how she and Jeff, the only other student at Halloway who was gay and "out," had decided, based partially on a lesson on civic engagement in Ms. Green's class, that they needed to create a student group that could be a "safe space" for LGBQ students. She shared that Terrence and Hu, two of their classmates who identified as heterosexual but also were moved by the same lesson, also wanted to help start the GSA. "We've already started talking about how to help educate our peers about homophobia," Lorraine explained. "We've even looked at what the GSAs at other schools are doing."

"Wow! Sounds like you've done your homework on this," Ms. Green replied, still listening intently.

"It's a nationwide movement," Lorraine continued. "All of these GSAs are linked up. There are resource guides, workshops, and all sorts of opportunities."

"Yes, of course I'll be your sponsor!" Ms. Green said. Nothing excited her more than a group of students taking the reins and initiating these sorts of efforts. Usually students who came to her with these requests did so in search of her permission or with the assumption that Ms. Green would lead the charge. Lorraine wasn't seeking permission or a leader. Instead she was taking the lead, doing her due diligence, and clearing the necessary hurdles by identifying a faculty sponsor.

Ms. Green knew, of course, that Lorraine, Jeff, Terrence, and Hu were heading down a difficult road; that their efforts might be met with ridicule from some of their peers and calls to the school from angry parents. As usual, though, she thought, "If it's change you want . . ." and agreed to support them any way she could.

A few days later Ms. Livingsworth, Halloway's principal, visited Ms. Green in her classroom after school. At first she sounded supportive of the students' efforts. "I think it's great that these young people are taking some initiative," she said. "They're braver than I was at their age."

"Especially now, when we're seeing more and more bullying," Ms. Green replied.

"I do have a concern about this particular group, though," Ms. Livingsworth explained. "We talk all the time about being inclusive. I'm proud of that commitment. My fear is that by allowing a Gay–Straight Alliance, we might be alienating some of our more conservative families whose religious communities don't approve of homosexuality."

"Those families already feel welcome here in every other way," Ms. Green insisted. "The students are just trying to carve out a little space for themselves as people who care about ending discrimination."

Ms. Livingsworth nodded. "I commend them for that. But it's just not the right time for a GSA. Let's suggest that they start a Diversity Club instead. That way all students will feel included."

Ms. Green knew this news would devastate Lorraine. She felt horribly disappointed herself, but knew that when Principal

Livingsworth makes up her mind about these sorts of things, there is no use trying to reason with her. Eventually she would need to raise this issue again, but for now she needed to focus on breaking the news to Lorraine.

Questions

1 In your opinion, was Ms. Livingsworth's suggestion that Lorraine and her peers start a Diversity Club rather than a GSA a suitable one? Why or why not? How is a general Diversity Club different in nature from a GSA?

2 If you were in Ms. Green's shoes, would you have argued more vigorously in support of the GSA? If so, how?

3 How should Ms. Green communicate this news to Lorraine? Can you think of any way in which Ms. Green could support the students' efforts to create a safer community for themselves and their peers while also complying with Ms. Livingsworth's request?

Turn to page 149 to view the Points for Consideration for this case.

CASE 9.2: DATE AUCTION

During a student council meeting at Shadow Creek High School, Jonathan, the council president, introduced the possibility of hosting a fundraiser for a local youth homeless shelter. Historically, Shadow Creek High School's student body had been white and upper-middle class. The school was located in a predominantly affluent suburb 20 miles from a major metropolitan city. However, as Jonathan reminded his classmates, the school's student population was growing increasingly diverse racially and economically. "I hate that people think we're just a bunch of rich white kids," he said. "Here's something we can do to change that perception." The council voted in favor of hosting the fundraiser, hoping also that their efforts would raise awareness among their classmates of the growing problem of youth homelessness in the area.

Once the vote passed, council members eagerly began brainstorming fundraising ideas. Their advisor, Mr. Hanson, believed in students taking ownership of their own projects, so he asserted his voice minimally during meetings. He listened to their conversation intently, but provided only occasional guidance.

One student, Tanya, suggested holding a "Date Auction" in which students could bid on an opportunity to go on a date with members of the senior class. Tanya had read online about another high school that had hosted a similar event. "It generated a *lot* of money," she explained, "and cost next to nothing." She added that the dates could be arranged to happen simultaneously in a local restaurant, ensuring student safety and mitigating any discomfort participants might experience. Another student, Terry, wondered aloud whether the restaurant could donate the meals so that all of the money they raised through the auction could be donated to the shelter. The students continued to discuss and plan the event with great enthusiasm. Rarely had they so quickly agreed on a program idea. "Our classmates are going to love this!" Jonathan said to a chorus of nods.

When the time came to identify volunteers who would be willing to be auctioned off and who would generate a lot of bidding interest, Tanya recommended Nate, a male student council member. "Everyone knows Nate and, more importantly, everybody *loves* Nate," Tanya said smiling. Nate agreed, joking that he would win the highest bids.

Chris, one of Nate's best friends, added that Nate would probably get bids "from girls *and from guys*" who would want a date with him, eliciting laughs from several of the students in the room.

Nate responded, "Whatever! I'm not gay. Even if it's for charity, I'm quitting if a guy bids on me. That's just *wrong!*" While some council members continued to laugh, others changed the topic to restaurants that might be willing to donate meals.

As planning was wrapping up and the meeting was coming to a close, Tanya asked Mr. Hanson if it would be all right for the student council to stipulate that bids would only be considered if made by "students of the opposite sex from the students we're auctioning off." She hoped that this stipulation would help them "avoid that kind of situation."

The council members looked at Mr. Hanson, waiting for a response.

Questions

1 At which point, if at all, should Mr. Hanson have intervened in this meeting? Why? How?

2 When Chris teased Nate about how he likely would get bids from women and men, some students laughed, but others did not. Why might some students not have found Chris's teasing or Nate's response funny?

3 In what ways might the idea of a Date Auction encourage gender bias and inequity? Did you see any evidence of this in the students' conversation?

4 In what ways might the idea of a Date Auction encourage homophobia, heterosexism, and heteronormativity? Did you see any evidence of this in the students' conversation?

5 Among Shadow Creek High School's students, who might be most offended by the council's idea? Who might feel most alienated by it?

Turn to page 150 to view the Points for Consideration for this case.

CASE 9.3: OUTED AT SCHOOL

Mr. Brooks, a middle school history teacher, never intended to move back to his hometown, a very conservative place where gay men like him were reminded constantly that they were not welcome. His mother had been diagnosed with cancer, though, so he moved home to care for her. Luckily, Ridge Rock Middle School, just a 15-minute drive from his mother's home, had an opening for a history teacher.

When he was offered the position by Ms. Patterson, the principal, he decided, reluctantly, to mention his sexual orientation. "I'm telling you this," he explained, "because I know this can be a rough environment for people like me. I can handle it. I have a lot of practice. But what I can't handle is not having the support of the administration."

"Wow, OK," Ms. Patterson responded, leaning back in her chair. "It's not every day somebody divulges his sexual identity after an interview. But since you brought it up, do you mind me asking how you'll handle it with your students?"

"If you're asking me whether I'll be 'out' at work, the answer is *no way*. Not here."

What Mr. Brooks did not know was that Ms. Patterson had been one of only a few heterosexual allies of lesbian, gay, bisexual, and queer-identifying (LGBQ) staff and students in the district. She knew there were at least two other LGBQ teachers at the school, which is to say two Ridge Rock teachers had come out to her. Neither was out to the rest of the school. Of course, she couldn't divulge that fact to Mr. Brooks without betraying the trust of those teachers. "If you're looking for my support, you have it," she said. "Let's just keep in touch about it and if you need anything my door is always open."

This brought Mr. Brooks a bit of relief. Still, when he remembered his experience as a closeted gay student in the area schools, he shuddered. Memories weighed on him of his classmates' *constant*, as he remembered it, use of words like "homo" and phrases such as "that's so gay," and the bullying doled out to students who did not conform to traditional gender identities, whether or not they identified as LGBQ. Worse, though, were the memories of unresponsiveness on the parts of many of the adults in his schools. He felt a little foolish for holding on to these concerns. *Maybe things have changed*, he thought, before remembering the sneers he and his partner, Steve, faced at a local restaurant last time he was home to visit his mother.

The first several months of the school year went surprisingly smoothly. Mr. Brooks heard the occasional offensive comment from students and the usual heteronormative assumptions—like asking him whether he had a girlfriend—from colleagues and students, but all in all it was friendlier than he had anticipated. He hated having to hide who he was, so the smoothness was a relative kind of smoothness, but given his initial concerns, relative smoothness felt like a small victory.

Then, in the middle of the final period of school in early December, Mr. Brooks was stunned when Jeremy, an eighth grader and one of his more boisterous students, asked him in front of the class whether he was gay. This was not a new question for him, so the asking itself did not faze him so much as the collective gasp of Jeremy's classmates. He knew what he *should* say: *That is not an appropriate thing to ask your teacher*. Instead, conscious that he might be opening up a can of worms, he calmly asked, "Why would you ask me that?"

"My brother told me. He saw it on Facebook," Jeremy said.

"How many of you have heard about this?" Mr. Brooks asked the class. About a third of his 27 students raised their hands. "This is not an appropriate thing for us to talk about at school," he said. "We will not discuss my personal life. Now let's focus on today's lesson."

Mr. Brooks was disappointed with how he'd handled Jeremy's question. Part of him wished he had said, "Yes. I'm gay and it makes me sad to think how much better of a teacher I could be for all of you if I didn't have to spend energy hiding it." Then he remembered where he was and how he needed that job.

When students left for the day he went to see Ms. Patterson. "Guess what happened today," he said.

"I can only guess," Ms. Patterson responded. "I've received several phone calls this afternoon. It seems a couple of high school students outed you on Facebook. Word got to parents. Some have called me to request I move their children out of your class."

"And what did you say?" Mr. Brooks queried.

"I said that your sexual orientation, whatever it is, is irrelevant to your teaching," she replied, "I told them you're an outstanding teacher and I refused to move their children."

"I appreciate that. So, what now?" Mr. Brooks asked. "I cannot lie about this to my students. Hiding it is one thing, but lying about it is something else."

"I wouldn't ask you to lie about it," Ms. Patterson said, "so let's figure this out together."

Questions

1 In your opinion, should Jeremy be punished for asking Mr. Brooks about his sexual orientation? Why or why not?
2 Although things were better at first than Mr. Brooks had anticipated, he still was subject to "heteronormative assumptions." In a heteronormative context, people are assumed to be heterosexual and heterosexuality is deemed "normal," even if implicitly so. What are some of the ways in which you have witnessed heteronormativity in schools?

3 How, if at all, should Mr. Brooks address the rumors with his students? To what extent should attitudes in the broader community dictate how he handles the situation?

4 Ms. Patterson so far has defended Mr. Brooks, insisting to complaining parents that his sexual orientation is irrelevant to his teaching. Should she do more? If so, what?

Turn to page 151 to view the Points for Consideration for this case.

CASE 9.4: TWO MOMS

Ms. Ribiero, a second grade teacher at Gibson Elementary School, was no big fan of controversy or conflict, but she was very attuned to her students' needs and equally committed to building authentic community in her classroom. So when she learned that Denise, who lived with her two mothers, would be in her class, she did some research and found two highly recommended books that depicted families with same-sex parents to add to her classroom library. She had no intention of teaching a lesson on same-sex partners or reading the book aloud or anything that might upset some of her other students' families. She just thought as a simple matter of inclusion that the books ought to be available to Denise and her classmates. She mentioned this to Denise's moms at Back to School Night. They were appreciative of her thoughtfulness.

Several months into the school year, Ms. Ribiero noticed a few students picking one of the books up and looking it over before putting it back and choosing something else to read. Then, one day in mid-November, she noticed Denise reading one of the books. Julia, one of Denise's classmates, was sitting next to her. "What are you reading?" Julia asked Denise.

"This," Denise replied, showing her Julia the book cover. "It's called *Emma and Meesha My Boy: A Two-Mom Story*."

"What's it about?"

Without skipping a beat Denise replied, "It's about a little girl who lives with her two moms and they have a cat." Ms. Ribiero, overhearing their conversation, walked slowly toward them.

"Two moms?" Julia asked, voice elevated, eliciting the attention of several other students who were reading nearby. "You mean she has two moms who live together? That's weird."

Brandon, another student sitting nearby looked up at Ms. Ribiero and, as if telling on her, pointed to Denise and said, "*She's* reading a book about weird people."

"OK Julia and Brandon," Ms. Ribiero interrupted, "focus on your own books and let Denise focus on hers."

Immediately Ms. Ribiero was dissatisfied with her response. She was uneasy, as usual, about doing anything that might seem too controversial. She definitely did not feel comfortable trying to teach a mini-lesson on family diversity or same-sex partners on the spot, nor did she feel prepared to do so. She agonized that evening over what to do. She knew she needed to do *something*, not as a matter of marriage rights or explicit advocacy for lesbian or gay people, but as a simple matter of accuracy. Families with two moms *do exist*. Although as far as she knew Denise was the only student in her class with same-sex parents, others lived in one of many other family structure scenarios.

Despite her uneasiness, Ms. Ribiero decided to read *Emma and Meesha My Boy* aloud to the class the following day. She wondered for a moment whether she should wait and maybe even send home notices so families could opt their children out of the activity if they wanted to do so, but she figured because she was using the book to begin a conversation about family diversity rather than "gay marriage" or "gay rights," the controversy would be averted.

She was thrilled the next day to see how open and curious her students were about the book. "So your family is like that?" Julia asked Denise.

"Yes. Two moms, and no dad," Denise replied, holding up two fingers.

As other students began asking Denise questions, Ms. Ribiero felt tempted to stop the conversation and remind them that there are many forms of family diversity. But she paused, proud of how respectful the students were being with one another and how empowered Denise appeared as she answered their questions. They did go on, after a while, to talk about other forms of family diversity, about living with grandparents, single parents or guardians, extended or joint families, and a foster family. Ms. Ribiero was thrilled with how it went.

She was thrilled, that is, until the next morning, when she learned from Principal Hernandez that several parents had called him complaining that she was teaching about "homosexuality" and "gay marriage" in class. "You know me and controversy," Ms. Ribiero said, "and you know I was not teaching about homosexuality or gay marriage."

"I know, I know," Mr. Hernandez responded, "but several of these parents apparently talked with one another and are coming by the office after school today. Some already have asked to have their students moved to another class."

Filled with anxiety, Ms. Ribiero explained, "All I did was read a book about a little girl with two moms. Denise is in my class and her classmates had questions. In a year or two those questions are going to turn into bullying if we don't do something now."

"Well, I know you're the last person who would start a firestorm purposefully. And I know you need to get to your classroom before the students start arriving. Come down to the office right after school today. The parents are arriving around 3:45 and I would like you there. That will give us about half an hour to talk about a strategy."

"OK, thank you," Ms. Ribiero said nervously before heading to her classroom.

Questions

1 How else could Ms. Ribiero have responded when she saw Julia and Brandon giving Denise a hard time about reading a book about a child with two moms?

2 Other than reading that book to the class, what might Ms. Ribiero have done to engage her students in a conversation about diverse family structures? How might she have engaged them in a more direct conversation about families with same-sex parents or guardians?

3 During her conversation with Mr. Hernandez, Ms. Ribiero made the point that the students' questions will turn into bullying if the school does not find some way to address those questions. What responsibility do teachers and administrators have to educate students about diverse family structures such as families with same-sex parents or guardians? What responsibility do they have to educate students about discrimination on the basis of sexual orientation?

4 Did Mr. Hernandez do the right thing by inviting Ms. Ribiero into the conversation with the parents in the after school meeting? Why or why not? How should he and Ms. Ribiero respond to the parents' complaints?

Turn to page 152 to view the Points for Consideration for this case.

10

Cases on Language

CASE 10.1: STUDENT TRANSLATOR

"Wait up, Maria!" Mr. Clark shouted as he hurried to catch up with his fifth grader and her mother who were leaving school at the end of the day. Maria Montes usually walked home with her sister, a third grader at the school, but on this particular day they were delighted to find their mother waiting outside the school for them.

Mr. Clark had been trying to reach Maria's mother, Ms. Montes, to discuss discipline concerns he had about Maria. Several students complained to him that Maria was not including them in activities at recess. Others complained that Maria was calling them names. Maria denied the accusations, but Mr. Clark, who started paying closer attention to Maria's interactions with her classmates, witnessed a few incidents and wanted to let her parents know what was happening.

He wrote a note home but noticed a few days later that it was still in Maria's backpack, undelivered. Next he called her parents, but he knew they were just beginning to learn English, so he wasn't confident they would understand the message he left for them.

Maria's mom was receptive during their last conference, when an interpreter was present. As he jogged to catch up with her, Mr. Clark wondered how a conversation would go now, given the fact that he did not speak Spanish.

When he finally reached them, Mr. Clark shook Ms. Montes's hand and asked her if she had a few minutes to talk. "Yes," she replied, and Mr. Clark noticed that Maria's expression changed, probably out of concern that the conversation was not going to go well. Mr. Clark felt that asking Maria to interpret would not be a good idea since he was not sure she would translate accurately, given the topic of the conversation. He turned, instead, to Marcella, Maria's younger sister, who had developed a reputation for being a helpful and bright student, and asked her if she could translate for him. Marcella nodded and explained to her mother why Mr. Clark had stopped them.

After several minutes of conversation, slowed a bit by the translation process, Maria, Ms. Montes, and Mr. Clark agreed on an appropriate behavior plan for Maria. Mr. Clark was pleased with the impromptu meeting and its results. "Thank you, Marcella," he said, and told her how wonderful it was that she was so proficient with two languages and that she was willing to help him. He looked at Maria's mom and said, "You must be very proud of her. She's very smart!"

Marcella beamed. "I can help other teachers too," she said, shyly. Mr. Clark smiled and said he might need her help translating for her mother in the future.

Looking back up at Maria and Ms. Montes, Mr. Clark noticed that they appeared uncomfortable. Seeing this, he reassured them, "I'm sure next time we will have something good to report."

"I'll see you tomorrow, Maria," he said with a little wave, then headed back toward the school.

Mr. Clark felt satisfied about what he was able to accomplish in the short impromptu meeting. He felt confident that Ms. Montes would follow through on their agreement for at-home support. As a bonus, he felt good about empowering Marcella and praising her for her help. He was happy to know she would be a resource if he did not feel he could trust Maria to translate for her mother.

It's a win–win situation, he thought.

Questions

1 Why might Ms. Montes and Maria have grown uncomfortable with Mr. Clark's interaction with Marcella?

2 In your opinion, was it appropriate for Mr. Clark to stop Ms. Montes, Maria, and Marcella on their walk home from school in

order to have a conversation about Maria's behavior? Why or why not?

3 Was it appropriate for Mr. Clark to ask Marcella to be the interpreter for the conversation? Why or why not?

Turn to page 152 to view the Points for Consideration for this case.

CASE 10.2: ENGLISH ONLY

Ms. Mancini knew as long as she could remember that she wanted to teach mathematics and that she wanted to do so in a linguistically and ethnically diverse school. What she did not expect was to be teaching at the very same middle school, Potomac Middle School, she had attended a decade and a half earlier. When she attended Potomac, the students, like the teachers, were almost exclusively white. She could not remember a single classmate who spoke a language other than English at home.

A few years ago when she started substitute teaching there during breaks from college, Ms. Mancini was surprised to see how much things had changed. As the suburbs expanded, more and more immigrants were moving into the area, seeking the service jobs that inevitably follow suburban growth. By the time Ms. Mancini decided to apply for a job at Potomac, more than 20 percent of the students spoke languages other than English at home.

Ms. Mancini loved it. She often teamed with Ms. de Leon, who was a mathematics teacher with a Teaching English to Speakers of Other Languages endorsement. Ms. de Leon, in addition to speaking English, spoke fluent Spanish and always tried to learn a little bit of every language spoken by her students. Ms. Mancini only spoke English fluently but she, too, tried to learn a few words in each of the languages of her students who did not speak English at home.

Some things had not changed at the school. Several of Ms. Mancini's former teachers still taught there. It was not uncommon for Ms. Mancini to hear them and many of her other colleagues lament the changes to the student population or discuss the challenges of teaching in a school where they felt the students or their families were not learning English quickly enough. "They're *all* our students,"

Ms. Mancini would say, but, aside from Ms. de Leon, she found very few teachers willing to publicly back her support of English Language Learners (ELLs).

During a mid-year faculty meeting, a small group of teachers collectively introduced their concerns about "the ELLs." Ms. Ross was particularly outspoken. "It's one thing for those students to speak their languages in the hallways or at lunch, but I'm hearing it more and more in my classroom and it's a distraction!" she exclaimed.

"Exactly!" Mr. Thompson agreed. "They could be saying anything. The other students might think the ELL students are talking about them."

"They are probably just talking about the same things all the other students talk about," Ms. Mancini interjected, but she quickly was drowned out by what felt, to her, like years of pent-up frustration being released all at once from the other teachers.

"It's their parents," Ms. Ross said. "They don't see a need to learn English and that hinders their children's ability to learn English."

"I used to be one of those students," Ms. de Leon responded. "When you talk about *those kids* you're talking about me. And I can tell you, you are way off base."

Sensing tension, Mr. Sumpter, the principal of the school who was an English teacher when Ms. Mancini attended Potomac, stepped in. "OK, OK. I don't like how contentious this is getting. We're all colleagues here." He continued, explaining how he had been feeling pressure from "some people at the district office" to institute the same sorts of English-only policies that already were in place in several other area schools. "This wouldn't affect what they do in their free time or while they are receiving language services," he explained, "but it would mean—it *will* mean—that during classroom time, students will not be allowed to speak any language other than English." After a short pause he continued with a chuckle, "That is, unless they're in Spanish, French, or German class."

As many of Ms. Mancini's coworkers laughed and expressed relief, all she could do was think of her students. She knew their home languages were invaluable to them during class, having witnessed so often how ELL students who spoke the same language helped each other to understand concepts they might have been struggling to understand in English. She glanced at Ms. de Leon, who looked back at her and shook her head gently. "Are you saying this is what we're going to do?" Ms. Mancini asked, although she was afraid of what the answer would be.

"Starting next term, so that we have time to decide the best way to address noncompliance on students' parts," Mr. Sumpter answered.

Ms. Mancini knew this was bad policy. She knew it was going to hurt the English Language Learners in her classes and that it already was alienating Ms. de Leon. She wanted to find a way to reverse this policy decision. She also needed a plan for what she would do in her own classroom if the policy did go into effect. Could she follow a policy she knew would negatively affect student learning?

Questions

1 Why might some people find it threatening or discomforting when somebody is speaking a language they do not understand?
2 Should Ms. Mancini enforce the policy and support the administration's decision even though she believes this policy is bad for her students, or should she attempt to change her colleagues' minds? If you believe she should do the latter, how might she go about trying to do so?
3 Would you have reached out to Ms. de Leon following the faculty meeting? If so, how?
4 If you were in a school in which an English-only policy was instituted, how might you engage students in a conversation about the policy and its implications, recognizing that students from families who do not speak English at home could feel alienated by the policy?

Turn to page 153 to view the Points for Consideration for this case.

CASE 10.3: FAMILY NIGHT

Among all the grade-level teams at Crestwood Elementary School, the most collaborative one, by far, was the fifth grade teachers. The five team members met regularly, working together to address a wide variety of issues. So when they noticed, during several school-wide events earlier in the year, disproportionately low attendance among parents and guardians of English Language Learning (ELL) students, they met and decided to do something about it.

The fifth grade team decided to host a Family Night event on a weeknight in February and set about planning the evening, being mindful to find a variety of ways to entice as many parents and guardians to attend as possible. Snacks and student performances surely would draw a crowd, they figured. The teachers sent home fliers that had been translated into the languages spoken in the homes of each student. They even arranged for students to perform the songs they had learned in music class. Following the performance, the teachers planned a brief presentation about how to reinforce math concepts at home by utilizing Web sites and online resources. The entire event would last only 30 minutes, they decided, trying to be sensitive to the fact that many of their students' parents and guardians worked evening shifts or had other responsibilities that made long school events difficult to attend. The program was scheduled to begin at 7:00 p.m.

Mr. Nelson, one of the more veteran fifth grade teachers, hoped that his grade-level team would set an example for the rest of the school, demonstrating how to optimize family participation. He was excited to prove that if events were planned thoughtfully, attendance would increase. He even took it upon himself to create a handout about how to access online math tools.

The evening of the Family Night, several families began arriving shortly before the published start time. The teachers noticed, however, that most of them were the families who attended every school event. Five minutes after the scheduled start time, with several people seated and awaiting the performance, but other families not yet in attendance, the teachers decided to change the order of the program around, moving their discussion of home support for math learning to the beginning, to be followed by the student performance.

The teachers were relieved to see more and more families filing into the event as they were speaking, and by the end of their presentation, almost all of the families had arrived. *This is a great turnout*, thought Mr. Nelson, but he worried that so many of the families missed learning how to help their children with math. He and the other teachers noticed that several of the families of ELL students stood in the back of the cafeteria rather than joining other families in the rows of seats they had provided. Many were chatting. The students did not seem to notice, but several parents and guardians who were sitting and watching the students perform appeared to be growing frustrated with the background noise.

Around 7:40 p.m., ten minutes after the event was scheduled to end, many families who arrived after the event had started were still chatting. Ms. Stowe, one of the newer fifth grade teachers, noticed that several copies of the handout Mr. Nelson had created were left on the table, so she personally handed one to each of the adults who did not have one. She felt disappointed that when she gave them the handout, so few of the parents and guardians in attendance took time to ask questions about it. By 7:45 p.m. several of the teachers were walking around the cafeteria reminding the remaining families that the event had ended.

Once everybody had left, the teachers met briefly to discuss the evening. Ms. Stowe expressed her discontent over what she interpreted as many of the ELL parents and guardians showing disinterest in the handout. Other fifth grade teachers complained that the evening was not a success because many of the ELL families for whom the event primarily was intended arrived late and seemed more interested in their conversations than the presentation.

Mr. Nelson could tell that his coworkers were discouraged by the evening. He knew it would reinforce some of the stereotypes they and other teachers in his building already had about certain families. He also knew that the evening held an important lesson for the fifth grade team and the school, but he was not sure what that lesson was.

Questions

1 Do you agree with the teachers' conclusion that the evening was not a success? Why or why not?

2 The teachers were careful to try to alleviate some potential barriers to participation for ELL families, such as language. What else, if anything, might they have done to make the evening as engaging to the families as possible? What strategies have you used successfully to maximize participation in these sorts of events?

3 Why might some of the families have remained in the back of the cafeteria rather than joining other families in provided seats? Should the teachers have intervened when some of the seated families appeared frustrated with the noise from their conversations? If so, how?

4 One goal of the evening was to give the families strategies for providing additional mathematics help at home for their children. The teachers felt this goal was not met for certain families and they were frustrated about it. What are some other ways in which such a goal might be accomplished?

Turn to page 154 to view the Points for Consideration for this case.

11

CASES ON IMMIGRANT STATUS

CASE 11.1: AN ASSIGNED NICKNAME

It was the first day of the school year at Treetop Elementary School. Ms. Goodwin, a kindergarten teacher, enjoyed meeting all of her students as well as the parents and guardians who saw their kids into her classroom. She always felt a little anxious on the first day of school, but for a reason she never quite understood, the challenge of learning to pronounce all of her students' names was especially nerve-inducing to her. The student body at her school was becoming more ethnically and linguistically diverse each year, and she struggled to properly pronounce the names of some of her students. Fully aware of her struggles, she listened closely to how each child's name was pronounced by the family member who brought her or him to the classroom.

Once the parents and guardians had left she invited her students to sit in a circle on the floor. "Let's learn a little bit about each other," she said, before asking them to share their names and favorite animals. When each student said their name, Ms. Goodwin repeated it, a strategy for learning names as quickly as possible. Despite her attentiveness, Ms. Goodwin found herself stumbling over the name of one of her students, a girl named Sarai (pronounced Să-ră-ē), whose family had immigrated from Mexico just before she was born.

Over the next few days Ms. Goodwin noticed that she was avoiding saying Sarai's name. She felt bad, but was not sure what to do. She decided to ask Sarai for help. Sarai tried to help, saying her name slowly, but as Ms. Goodwin continued to struggle pronouncing it, she sensed that Sarai was growing uncomfortable.

Another of Ms. Goodwin's students, Sara, was standing nearby. She looked at Sarai and exclaimed, "Our names are almost the same! Maybe you can be called Sara too."

"Ok," Sarai replied tentatively. Ms. Goodwin asked Sarai if she was sure this would be OK. Sarai nodded, and Ms. Goodwin ended the conversation by saying, "That's fine. Sara is a pretty name."

For the next several weeks Sarai was introduced, and introduced herself, to students and staff as "Sara."

When it came time for conferences, Ms. Goodwin, momentarily forgetting that "Sara" was not Sarai's given name, noticed some confusion on her mother's face when she referred to her as "Sara." She explained to Sarai's mother that some of the students have nicknames and that they prefer to be called by those names. "Sarai said it was fine to call her 'Sara'," she said. "Is that OK with you?"

Sarai's mother nodded, and Ms. Goodwin continued with the conference. She noticed, however that Sarai's mother seemed quieter and less engaged than earlier.

Questions

1 What other strategies could Ms. Goodwin have used to learn to pronounce Sarai's name correctly?

2 It is possible that Sarai agreed to change her name even if she did not really want to be called "Sara." Why might this be the case? Why might her mother have assented even if she was not completely comfortable with her daughter being called "Sara"?

3 How might Ms. Goodwin have introduced the topic of Sarai's nickname in a way that invited her mother to share concerns she might have had? When should she have invited Sarai's parents or guardians into such a conversation?

4 Why is it so important for teachers to learn to pronounce every student's full given name correctly? Does this depend on whether the student asks to be called by a name that might be easier to pronounce?

Turn to page 155 to view the Points for Consideration for this case.

CASE 11.2: I'M NOT BLACK

Ms. Lee, a history teacher at Fairfield Middle School, valued the growing racial and religious diversity of her students. There were some tensions in the larger community, and sometimes those tensions managed to find their way into the school; but for the most part it appeared to her as though students got along very well. There were few reported incidents of racial or religious bias or bullying.

In fact, Ms. Lee often attempted to create opportunities for students to collaborate in pairs or small groups in order to help facilitate relationship-building across racial and ethnic groups in her classes. She watched happily as her students—a combination predominately of Native American, white, and African American students, and a small but slowly growing population of students whose parents recently came to the U.S. as political refugees from Nigeria—discussed historical narratives or complex political issues together, learning from one another's perspectives.

Recently, though, Ms. Lee and her colleagues began noticing what appeared to be steadily growing conflict at the school that surprised them: conflict between the Nigerian students and African American students. A few brief shoving incidents between individual Nigerian and African American students had broken out over the last week or so, and social divisions between the groups were becoming more pronounced.

Late in February a new student, Abiola, was assigned to Ms. Lee's fourth-period class. His family had been in the U.S. for three years but had just moved to the area so his father could join his uncle in opening a small Nigerian market. Although Ms. Lee had at least one Nigerian student in most of her classes, Abiola became the only Nigerian student in her fourth-period class. Ms. Lee, as she always did for students who joined her classes mid-term, decided to assign Abiola a "mentor"—a fellow student who could help him follow class routines and be a supportive presence in other ways. Hoping to build a bridge between the African American and Nigerian students, she asked Warren, one of her African American students, to stay after class so that she could introduce them formally.

It did not go as planned. "I didn't know you were asking me to stay after school for *this*," Warren said. "You know the other Nigerian kids have been calling us names like the n-word, right?" Abiola stood motionless, eyes cast downward, hands stuffed into his jean pockets.

"What?" Ms. Lee responded, a puzzled look on her face. "Why? That doesn't make any sense."

"They think they're better than us," Warren explained. "They think they're not black."

"I'm not 'black'," Abiola said softly, "I'm Nigerian. I don't need his help."

Ms. Lee replied, "OK. Well, you young men need to learn how to get along because I won't have any of this squabbling in my classroom. I want you to shake hands."

Barely making eye contact, Warren and Abiola quickly shook hands.

Later that afternoon, after the school day had ended, a small group of young Nigerian men got into a shoving match with a group of young African American men in the school parking lot. The melee was broken up before any punches were thrown, but tensions between the groups remained high.

Speaking with a couple of her colleagues about the incident, Ms. Lee said, "I can't understand it. I know there are always social tensions with kids this age, but they're all black, right? You would think they would get along better because they have that in common. "

"I agree," replied Mr. Werth, "but whatever the issue, we need to find a solution before this turns into a full blow-out."

"Well I *do* understand it," replied Ms. Thompkins, one of the few African American teachers at the school. "We contribute to the tension by treating the students like they are all the same when they don't see it that way. These tensions are not unique in our country's history."

Ms. Lee considered Ms. Thompkins's points carefully, reflecting on her own experience as an immigrant.

After a moment, Mr. Werth interrupted her reflection. "So you're saying *we're* the problem here?" he asked. "I always try to not see the differences in my students and instead to see the commonalities. They should do the same."

Ms. Lee knew she had more work to do to understand the complexities of the tensions between the African American and Nigerian students, but something about what Mr. Werth had just said did not feel quite right to her. Of course, she wished all her students would find a way to get along, but she also wondered what she could do differently to quell the tensions.

Questions

1 What factors should Ms. Lee have taken into consideration when choosing a mentor for Abiola?

2 What, if anything, should Ms. Lee have done differently to address Warren's concerns and to ensure that Abiola felt welcomed?

3 Mr. Werth expressed a color-blind mentality when he said that he tries to see only the commonalities among his students. How might a color-blind approach affect his ability to understand and address the situation at hand?

4 What did Ms. Thompkins mean when she explained that "These tensions are not unique in our country's history"? What examples from the history of the United States might she have been thinking about? Can you think of an example of tension or bias between white citizens and one or more groups of recent white immigrants in United States history?

Turn to page 155 to view the Points for Consideration for this case.

CASE 11.3: A LEGACY OF PRIVILEGE ON THE SOCCER FIELD

The women's varsity soccer team at Park Heights High School had a rich legacy, having won several state championships. Among the sports for which the school had both a women's team and a men's team, soccer was the only one for which the women's games drew more spectators than the men's games. Mr. Rosenthal, the team's coach of eight years, was proud of the consistent success of the team and never missed an opportunity to remind his players of it.

What had become a little less consistent, though, was the racial make-up of the team. Until five or six years ago, Park Heights had been a predominantly white school and the athletic teams reflected these demographics. Slowly, however, this was changing as greater numbers of Mexican and Salvadoran families, mostly undocumented immigrants, had begun moving into the area. At first the children of these families were hesitant to participate in organized extracurricular school activities, including athletics, so a local community organization started a youth soccer league. Most people in the community expected the men's part of the league to flourish and were a little surprised to see so many girls—especially Mexican and Salvadoran young women—express interest in playing. Little by little, these young women were trying out for, and making, the Park Heights varsity soccer team.

The previous season, of the 18 young women on the team, 7 were Latina and 11 were white. Mr. Rosenthal and Ms. Ferris, the principal of Park Heights, received several phone calls from parents of white students who complained of the "changing face" of the girls' soccer team. This season was the first in which there was a real possibility that the team would become majority Latina players. There was much chatter about this among some of the white parents in the community. This chatter was elevated, though, when Save Park Heights, a local organization created to pressure local legislators into passing laws to deny undocumented immigrants access to public services, including public schools, began publishing a blog and op-eds. These publications usually involved references to the girls' soccer team as an illustration of how, in their words, "real citizens are losing opportunities to illegals." Mr. Rosenthal largely steered clear of the public debate, except to repeat, whenever contacted by the media, that their job was to give each student in the school equal access to every opportunity.

Ms. Ferris hated controversy. This made Mr. Rosenthal a little nervous, especially when he learned that a group of white parents, whose daughters had played soccer for years and intended to try out for the soccer team, came to the school to meet with the principal.

"What do you plan to tell them?" he asked.

"I only plan on listening," she replied, "and then we'll meet and I'll fill you in."

Later, when Mr. Rosenthal and Ms. Ferris met, she let him know that the parents threatened to work with Save Park Heights to protest the women's soccer games and direct negative press to the school if they didn't do something to "reverse the trend."

"So what does that mean?" Mr. Rosenthal asked. "The players try out. The assistant coaches and I choose the best players. I'm not getting into politics about immigration. All I can do is choose the best players who try out."

Ms. Ferris responded, "I hear you. On the other hand, if they do protest and heighten the controversy, it could hurt *all* of our immigrant students. We can't afford the controversy."

"What are you asking me to do?" Mr. Rosenthal inquired.

"Just try to keep things even," his principal replied. "Doesn't that sound reasonable?"

"You mean, however tryouts go, make sure I don't give more than half the spots on the team to Mexican and Salvadoran players? How do we explain that to *their* families?" Mr. Rosenthal asked, exasperated.

"Well," Ms. Ferris said, "do what you need to do to avoid this controversy. As for the Mexican and Salvadoran families, they're not speaking up. All I can do is to respond to the families who are speaking up."

Suddenly Mr. Rosenthal was not looking forward to soccer tryouts the following week. He had his orders, but he knew they were unjust, even to the white players.

Questions

1 How should Ms. Ferris have responded to parents of white students who insisted that the trend of changing demographics on the women's soccer team "be reversed"?

2 Ms. Ferris mentioned that the Mexican and Salvadoran families were not speaking up about the controversy surrounding the women's soccer team. Why might they have been hesitant to speak up? Do you agree with Ms. Ferris's assessment that she should not have considered their concerns because they were not speaking up? Why or why not?

3 Should Ms. Ferris or Mr. Rosenthal have taken more of a public stand on the issue of educational access for the students at Park Heights who were undocumented immigrants? Why or why not?

4 What should Mr. Rosenthal do, knowing that what Ms. Ferris is requesting of him is unjust?

Turn to page 156 to view the Points for Consideration for this case.

CASE 11.4: PARENT INVOLVEMENT

Joel Pham was a fourth grader in Mr. Rolnick's class at Park Elementary School. Joel's parents reliably attended conferences and returned permission slips, but that was the extent of their involvement when it came to visiting the school.

Joel's mother, Ms. Pham, worked at QuickPrint, a local printing company that was known for encouraging its employees to do community service. The company even offered to pay its employees to volunteer during designated work days throughout the year. Most QuickPrint employees whose children attended Park Elementary would come to school on these days and do whatever school staff needed them to do. Ms. Pham, however, never visited the school during QuickPrint's service day.

Like many teachers, Mr. Rolnick believed that family involvement was integral to student success, so he constantly tried to provide opportunities for parents and guardians to volunteer during and after school. The school prided itself on its high levels of family volunteerism and almost all of the parents and guardians of Mr. Rolnick's students participated in some way, except for those who worked multiple jobs and simply could not afford to take time off from work. Mr. Rolnick was sensitive to their challenges.

He was somewhat perturbed, though, that Joel's parents, who to his knowledge had no such limitations, did not make much of an effort or show much interest in being involved. Mr. Rolnick knew that transportation was not an issue for them. The family lived within walking distance of the school. He knew Joel and his parents were ethnically Vietnamese, but Ms. and Mr. Pham were raised in the United States. In fact, they both completed their K–12 schooling in the school district that included Park Elementary, so language was not a barrier.

Mr. Rolnick often sent letters home with students in which he detailed in-school family involvement opportunities such as shelving books in the library or updating bulletin boards. Understanding that some parents and guardians might want to be involved but have difficulty getting to the school, he also included work-from-home opportunities, such as preparing materials for school events such as the carnival and bake sale. Joel's parents never responded to these letters.

When Mr. Rolnick mentioned volunteer opportunities during conferences, Ms. and Mr. Pham politely declined. Several weeks later, when Joel expressed an interest in working with a classmate, Myles, for the upcoming Science Fair, Mr. Rolnick said he would need to speak to the parents first. He called Mr. Pham and suggested that the boys, the teacher, and a parent from each family meet to come up with a plan that would ensure both boys had equal responsibilities and that the level of detail would justify two people working together. Mr. Rolnick said his schedule was flexible, but Mr. Pham said that he would speak with Joel at home and send in their plan. After hanging up the phone, Mr. Rolnick shook his head in disbelief, feeling that, yet again, Joel's parents could not be bothered to come to the school.

Exasperated, he decided to talk about his concern with a coworker whom he met in the staff lounge as he was headed home. This coworker, Ms. Smith, had taught in the school for more than 20 years and often offered advice to other teachers. "I've reached out to the Phams on several occasions," Mr. Rolnick explained. "I even called to invite them to a meeting with another parent and said I could meet at a time that works for them, but Mr. Pham refused, saying only that he'd handle it at home."

"OK," Ms. Smith said after learning more about Mr. Rolnick's frustrations. "I don't want to speak for them," she continued, "but I do encourage you to think a little bit about the reasons why they might not want to spend time in the school. I remember Joel's parents and recall that they attended this school when there were very few Vietnamese families in the area. Unfortunately, the school did not provide a welcoming environment, though we tried, and I am sure they were happy to move on. Some of the same teachers are here— teachers who never seemed very interested in them. Perhaps that has something to do with their reluctance."

"I'm not one of those teachers," Mr. Rolnick said, a little offended that he was being lumped in with teachers who might have been biased a couple of decades ago.

"No, you're not," Ms. Smith replied. "But might the assumptions you're making or the way you're approaching the Phams remind them of some of those teachers? Have you not begun with the assumptions that something is wrong with *them*, which is what they experienced and saw their own parents experiencing when they were students here?"

Mr. Rolnick closed his eyes and sighed. "Maybe you're right," he conceded.

"Well, let's focus on the task at hand," Ms. Smith said. "Let's talk about some different strategies for making Ms. and Mr. Pham feel welcome in the school."

"Yes, let's do that," said Mr. Rolnick, thankful for Ms. Smith's willingness to help.

Questions

1 Mr. Rolnick provided various opportunities for his students' parents to volunteer, but Ms. and Mr. Pham did not volunteer in these capacities. Ms. Smith suggested that one reason for their lack of participation might be their own experience as students in the school. What other factors might be keeping them from volunteering?

2 Is parent involvement an essential component to student success? How would you describe the nature of the "involvement" Mr. Rolnick was seeking?

3 How should Mr. Rolnick and other teachers and administrators reach out to parents and guardians who might have experienced school as a hostile environment when they were students?

4 Mr. Rolnick appeared to assume that, because they didn't take advantage of the family involvement opportunities he created, Ms. and Mr. Pham were uninvolved or disinterested in their son's education. What are some ways in which parents and guardians can be involved and demonstrate interest in their children's education other than volunteering at the school?

Turn to page 157 to view the Points for Consideration for this case.

CASE 11.5: MY UNCLE

Abdi was an energetic third grader who excelled academically. He was well liked by his peers, but their patience toward him was diminishing because he increasingly needed to be reminded to stop talking and to pay attention. Ms. Klein, his teacher, had noticed his tendency to talk a lot and to be distracted even before the school year began, during the "Meet Your Teacher" family night. Abdi's excitement for school was obvious, but despite instructions from his mother to wait his turn and listen to the teacher, he had difficulty following directions. It wasn't until his father sternly reprimanded him that evening that his behavior changed. Upon seeing this, Ms. Klein knew that Abdi was *capable* of following school rules, but that he needed guidance.

As she was planning for conferences in November, Ms. Klein made sure to remind Abdi that his mother and father should attend. She wanted to discuss Abdi's behavior with his parents in person because she did not want them to misinterpret her concerns and think that Abdi was being disrespectful or mean. Instead, she wanted them to understand that he struggled to stop talking when he should be listening, and that his behavior was becoming a distraction for the other students. She also hoped that Adbi's father would attend, believing that he would address the behavior concerns effectively.

When Abdi's designated conference time arrived, his mother, Ms. Asha, entered Ms. Klein's classroom with a man whom Ms. Klein assumed was an interpreter. Though Abdi's parents were immigrants from Somalia, Ms. Klein wondered why an interpreter would be present, as Ms. Asha spoke English very well. Ms. Klein learned that her assumption was incorrect when the man introduced himself as Abdi's uncle. After hearing Ms. Klein's concerns, they agreed to speak to Abdi at home about his conduct in class. Ms. Klein, feeling skeptical that this would take care of the issue, suggested that they also inform Abdi's father about his behavior. Ms. Asha and Abdi's uncle casually replied that they would convey the information, but Ms. Klein wondered whether they were saying so only to appease her.

The conference ended early, so after saying goodbye to Abdi's mother and uncle, Ms. Klein went to the main office to check her mailbox. "You look a little frustrated," the administrative assistant, Ms. Larson, mentioned. "Is everything going OK with conferences?"

"Things are fine," Ms. Klein replied. "I *am* a little frustrated, though." She scanned the office to make sure nobody else was around before adding, "I just finished Abdi's conference and I was really hoping to speak with his father about Abdi's behavior, but he didn't come. Instead, Abdi's mom and some guy who said he was Abdi's uncle came, and I don't have much confidence that either of them will talk to Abdi or be able to influence him to be better behaved in class. Abdi's so bright. He just needs to learn how to follow directions."

"Abdi is a sweet kid, very friendly," Ms. Larson said. "As for the uncle, well, I've seen several people over the years arrive after school to pick up Abdi, claiming to be his aunt or uncle. To be honest, I don't think any of them are related. I've seen the same thing with other immigrant students. It's a big problem if the adults are claiming to be somebody they are not."

Ms. Klein, shaking her head in disbelief, picked up her mail and said, "Well, I'll keep you posted if I learn anything new."

The next day, as the students were arriving and preparing for their morning routine, Ms. Klein noticed that Abdi was his usual talkative self. She walked over to him and casually said, "Good morning, Abdi. I had a good conference with your mom and uncle yesterday. It was nice to see your mom again."

Abdi smiled and said, "I worked on my homework when my mom was gone and I finished it all before she got back."

"That's great!" Ms. Klein replied. She then casually inquired, "It was nice for your uncle to come, too. Is he your mom's brother or your dad's brother?"

Abdi, looking puzzled and embarrassed, replied, "Neither," then walked away to join a group of his peers.

Ms. Klein sighed and thought to herself, *I'll have to let Ms. Larson know she was right.* Then she walked to the front of her classroom and waited for the bell to ring to signify the start of the school day.

Questions

1 Based on Ms. Klein's observations, was Abdi's father's presence at conferences necessary? What are some possible reasons why somebody else from the family might attend meetings at the school in his place?

2 How might Ms. Larson's mistrust of certain visitors affect how she interacts with them?

3 Ms. Klein asked Abdi about his relationship with his uncle in order to gather more information regarding who attended the meeting with his mother. Based on Abdi's response, how, if at all, might that exchange affect his comfort level in the classroom and relationship with his teacher?

Turn to page 157 to view the Points for Consideration for this case.

APPENDIX A

THE EQUITY LITERACY CASE ANALYSIS WORKSHEET

Paul C. Gorski and Seema G. Pothini

Step 1: Identify the problem or problems posed by the case.

Step 2: Take stock of varying perspectives.

Step 3: Consider possible challenges and opportunities.

Step 4: Imagine equitable outcomes.

Step 5: Brainstorm immediate-term responses.

Step 6: Brainstorm longer-term policy and practice adjustments.

Step 7: Craft a plan of action.

APPENDIX B
POINTS FOR CONSIDERATION

Case 3.1: Chocolate Bar Fundraiser

- Voting, as a form of decision-making, captures the majority desire but does not always result in an equitable decision. Sometimes we have to support an unpopular course of action because it's the equitable thing to do, even if a majority of people disagree with it.

- This case provides an important opportunity to discuss how PTA meetings and other opportunities for in-school family involvement are often not as accessible to low-income families as they are to middle-class or wealthier families. Low-income parents or guardians are more likely than their wealthier peers to work multiple jobs, including evening jobs, and are less likely to be able to afford child care or public transportation if they are necessary in order to participate. So although it can be easy to interpret the lower levels of some types of school involvement by low-income families as an indication that they don't care enough about school, we might ask ourselves, instead, how we might make opportunities for school involvement more accessible to low-income families.

- Mr. Winterstein provides a good example of what often is called the "deficit perspective," suggesting that lower-income kids could sell just as many chocolate bars as their peers if they just worked harder. The problem with the deficit perspective is that it ignores context, like the inability for poor families to afford to buy a large percentage of their children's chocolate bar allotment. Being an equitable and just educator means, in part, being able to recognize the deficit perspective and refusing to contribute to it by blaming low-income youth for the results of their poverty.

- Parent groups such as the PTA play an important role in schools. Although some PTAs are viewed simply as a means to bring volunteers to the building or to fundraise, it is important to realize the collective power such a group can have. These groups can make a significant impact upon their schools by contacting local elected officials such as school board members, mayors, and state representatives and expressing their concerns over school funding. Setting aside meeting time to learn about advocacy, changes in funding or policy, as well as the changing demographics can help the group to be more effective when making decisions and reaching out to others.

Case 3.2: A Class Lesson in Etiquette

- It's important to remember that families, depending on their socioeconomic statuses, might not have access to the same material resources as their wealthier peers. This does not make them less civilized, but it does mean they are less likely, on average, to have, say, separate salad or dessert forks, cloth napkins, or other pieces of formal place settings, just as they might be less likely to have computers at home or materials for some types of science projects. They are also less likely than their wealthier counterparts to have a separate dining table or to have work schedules that facilitate formal family meals. Again, this is not a matter of civility, but of material wealth.

- We should be careful not to put low-income students in a position in which they are forced to *perform* their economic disadvantage. When we do create a learning opportunity for low-income students that potentially puts them in such a position, we should be vigilant in our efforts to build on their experiences and cultures rather than sending a message, however implicitly, that they are being compared against people who are more privileged than they are. Tanya's response, in addition to being a keen observation about how privilege was playing out in Mr. Peyton's classroom, also might have been her way of pushing back against Ms. Hollingsworth's suggestion that her and her classmates' eating habits were not acceptable. (It's likely that Ms. Hollingsworth would struggle similarly to adjust to the etiquette standards if immersed suddenly into a cultural context with which she was unfamiliar, such as one in which eating utensils are not used at all.)

- There is merit in the idea of helping students to learn the behaviors that are valued in different social and cultural contexts, as well as teaching students how to adjust their behavior depending on the situation so that they are able to function successfully in multiple environments. There is less merit, however, in the idea that the "dining etiquette" being taught by Ms. Hollingsworth is inherently superior to any other common dining practices. In some cultural contexts, for instance, the primary standards of dining etiquette are built around sharing food and the fellowship that occurs when people eat together. In those cases, the precise placement of a dessert fork is not particularly important. Eating with one's hands is also culturally appropriate in many cultures. When we introduce to students cultural practices that might be different from their own, we should be cautious not to communicate, even unintentionally, that what they are learning is superior to their families' cultural practices.

Case 3.3: Student Protest

- Students who are denied equitable educational opportunity are often very conscious of the inequities they are experiencing. It only is natural that they would look for ways to respond. Unfortunately, when youth who experience any sort of inequity respond, even in the most peaceful and constructive ways, they are commonly viewed as troublemakers. This case provides an important opportunity to reflect on the subtle and not so subtle ways in which people might be seen as troublemakers simply for advocating for educational equity.

- Walkouts are a common form of student protest. School administrators and local law enforcement officials often respond to student walkout plans by increasing police officer presence in schools. In essence, by doing so, they increase tensions in the short term and criminalize student self-efficacy in the long term.
- School closings often take place in neighborhoods that already are blighted by a number of other challenges, including declining infrastructure, high foreclosure rates, and a lack of services such as banks and hospitals. Declining enrollment often occurs as a result of these kinds of external factors. It is important to consider the institutional factors that lead to school closures and attempt to address them proactively rather than reactively.

Case 3.4: High Expectations or Unrealistic Goals?

- This case showcases the reality that access and opportunity are often granted on the basis of one's existing levels of access and opportunity. As educators who are committed to providing their students with equitable opportunities, it is worthwhile considering what institutional factors in our schools and districts prohibit students from reaching their goals, including having access to higher education options upon completing high school.
- Although Ms. Sutter recognized Mr. Stein's comments as prejudicial, she did not have the same reaction when her peers said similar things during the staff meeting. Their comments might not have been as blatant as Mr. Stein's, but it is important to note that they were all biased. These types of negative assumptions, subtle or not, have the potential to influence how teachers approach daily instruction and interaction with their students. Research shows that teachers' expectations for students influence student outcomes tremendously. Consider what disservice and harm we do when we try to limit our students by what we perceive our society thinks is realistic for them.
- It is clear that students' parents were interested in supporting the club that Ms. Sutter created. Knowing this, Ms. Sutter might have collaborated with students' parents and guardians to

co-design the program, drawing on the conversations about college some of them already might have been having at home.

- It is important to remember that we present higher education as a series of options, careful to encourage students to think about those options without disparaging people who did not go to college or who are currently choosing not to pursue higher education. When we disparage people who do not pursue higher education, we are, in effect, disparaging the families of students who could become the first people in their families to attend college.

Case 4.1: The Winter Party

- It is important to distinguish between inclusivity and tokenism. Focusing primarily on Christmas-themed activities and then including one Hanukkah activity and, perhaps, a Kwanzaa activity is tokenism. Hanukkah, after all, traditionally is not a major Jewish holiday in the way that Christmas is a major Christian holiday. Notice, too, that the people who are planning this event never explicitly raise a question about what such a party would mean to students who do not celebrate Kwanzaa, Hanukkah, or Christmas, including students from a variety of religious and spiritual traditions that do not celebrate holidays at all or students whose families do not identify with any religion.
- Kwanzaa is not a religious holiday, but rather a celebration of African heritage and African American culture. Several mis-perceptions about this and other non-Christian holidays are perpetuated in schools. Some educators might be inclined to skip discussions of holidays in their classrooms because of a worry that some might be given more attention than others. While this attempt at being equitable may be rooted in good intentions, the impact might be negative because students are unable to share events that are honored or celebrated in their homes.
- Although Ms. Tate is happy that the volunteers are taking ownership of the party, it is important to note that the teachers are ultimately responsible for what is occurring in their

classrooms, including parties and celebrations. Sometimes the act of the democratic vote isn't actually the most "fair" decision for a group. While it may be easier for an educator to allow the "majority rules" parents to do some of the heavy lifting in the classroom or school, this often marginalizes parents whose voice is different, whose numbers are fewer, or who might be unable to be present to represent their viewpoint. Wealth and privilege are also made manifest by knowing you will be "heard" or seen as "normal," "part of the group." Asserting that something is "no big deal" is an act that those in a majority can use to assert privilege and to silence difference, since speaking up becomes inherently, then, "a big deal."

- This case provides an important opportunity to talk about the variety of ways in which Christianity is privileged in public schools. Although many public schools have become more conscious of not explicitly celebrating Christian holidays while ignoring or tokenizing those from other religious and spiritual traditions, there are many ways in which Christianity continues to be normalized in public schools. The simplest example might be the fact that "winter break" is scheduled around Christmas and "spring break" around Easter. Ms. Tyler's comment that Christmas is not religious, but American, is evidence of this normalization of Christianity.

Case 4.2: Christmas Lights?

- Because of Ms. Bren's own cultural view, she assumed the lights she saw were Christmas lights, not decorative lights. Around October and November, some religious holidays such as Diwali, the Hindu festival of lights, and Eid-al-Fitr, the celebration marking the end of Ramadan for Muslims, occur. People from these faiths, as well as others, may use strings of lights as decorations for their religious festivals. Others, regardless of their religion, simply might find the lights to be decorative without associating them with Christmas.

- Ms. Bren's students who were bothered by her tweet and her conversation with her colleague did not feel comfortable expressing why they were bothered. If students feel disengaged or disrespected, even the best content strategies or lesson plans can be ineffective. The danger then becomes attributing student performance in class as a reflection of their ability, rather than examining the environment created by the teacher which caused the student to become disengaged.

- We, as educators, should remember that students are constantly evaluating our actions during the school day, at school functions, and on social media. What is overheard between teachers or communicated through social media can have just as much impact as what students hear from a teacher standing at the front of a classroom. For this reason, it is critical to create and maintain a classroom environment where students can question or challenge a teacher, or their peers, without fearing negative repercussions.

Case 4.3: A Difference in Perspectives

- Mr. Ortiz was hesitant to educate members of the school community, including students in his homeroom class, about the positive significance of the symbol. This hesitation might stem from his lack of familiarity with religious symbols. However, by not addressing the situation more thoughtfully, he could be depriving students of a valuable lesson in critical thinking. As Madelyn demonstrated, students are eager to learn things that challenge their views and to share that knowledge with others.
- Mr. Ortiz told Nikhil that he should not wear the charm at school because of its potential to spark disruptions among students. Legal precedents suggest that school officials *can* censor religious and political expression if they can demonstrate or reasonably forecast that the expression will cause a *substantial* disruption to the school. This case provides an important opportunity to explore what constitutes a substantial disruption and how interpretations of "disruption" might change depending upon whose cultural symbols are at issue.
- There have been numerous cases in the United States of students being asked to remove religious symbols or articles of clothing in

schools because of dress code violations. Community reaction to these interventions has varied considerably from situations involving rosary beads to those involving hijab. Educators might be inclined to appeal to the majority voice, or to what they *believe* most people think. While this approach may seem sensible, it is rarely equitable. When we make decisions on the basis of appeasing the majority, we risk marginalizing people whose identities, like Nikhil's, are not in the majority.

Case 4.4: Islamophobic Read-Aloud

- Being equitable and just educators sometimes requires us to take a stand on issues such as Islamophobia. If we don't take a stand, even if we try to appear neutral, it can appear to students as though we are complying with the dominant or discriminatory view. In many ways, not responding is just as much a response as responding.
- This case provides an opportunity to discuss how important it is to be mindful of who our students are and how power is distributed among them. In this case, knowing George's reputation and the heaviness of the topic, Ms. McGrath might have been better off collecting the free writes and then picking one or two of them to share.
- Notice George's collective language—his use of "we" and "us." It is important to learn how to catch these subtle declarations of community agreement and to analyze who they really include. Obviously, in this case they do not include Hasina or Essam, and they probably don't include many other students in the room, so the very language in George's free write implicitly sets up an "us/them" dichotomy that cements their identities as "outsiders." We should be mindful of whether, even if unintentionally, we are contributing to similar types of insider/outsider dichotomies in the language we use.

Case 5.1: Generalizations on Display

- Ms. Lewis had good intentions when she displayed her students' projects, but the impact of the misinformation and generalizations can be harmful. In fact, failing to address these concerns with her students even harms her students, who are left with misunderstandings and simplistic thinking about the cultural and historical complexities of countries. It is important to learn how to recognize these sorts of learning opportunities when they present themselves and to take advantage of them.

- The fact that Ms. Whitney was the first person to mention the issues with some of the posters is not sufficient evidence that she was the first person to notice or be affected by those issues. Every student who looks at the posters, for example, is affected. It is important to remember that, for instance, some parents or guardians might not feel empowered to speak up when they see something in a school that offends them. They might fear negative repercussions for their children, or want to avoid being labeled as a trouble-maker, or, in the case of some immigrants, they might not feel confident enough with their English skills to speak up.
- It is important to regularly observe what is displayed on the walls in our schools to ensure that posters, advertisements, or student work is free of bias and inaccuracies such as those in the posters. Additionally, it is important to ensure that welcoming and engaging material that reflects the diversity and interests of the student population is displayed.

Case 5.2: Not Time for Stories

- Because Ms. Ward dismissed DeQuan's contribution as a story rather than an answer to her question, he and other students might get the idea that their contributions are not valued. Storytelling is a rich tradition in many families and might be a natural part of communication for some students. In some ways, his ability to make connections between various events and topics demonstrates a more advanced cognitive process than the kind for which Ms. Ward was asking. She could have seen in DeQuan's story descriptive words about California, such as "sunny" and "warm." These were the same words she recorded after hearing them from Madelyn.

- Ms. Ward validated Madelyn's contribution by saying that she was correct, perhaps indirectly communicating to DeQuan that he was incorrect. Ms. Ward also distanced herself from DeQuan by telling him he was being disrespectful when he might have thought she was being disrespectful by interrupting him. This provides an important opportunity to discuss the ways in which students' behavior can be as much a reflection of our own missteps as it is about them, and the humility it takes to consider that possibility.
- Ms. Ward's initial question limited responses to students who had traveled to California, which would have excluded and might have alienated students whose families could not afford such a trip.
- In an attempt to proactively avoid further disruption from DeQuan, Ms. Ward called out his potential behavior in front of the class, further embarrassing him. Though this case can be addressed in isolation, it is worthwhile considering the long-term effects of these micro-aggressions on student success in school. Furthermore, if Ms. Ward incorrectly views DeQuan's behavior as disrespectful, and this type of interaction between the two of them continues, DeQuan runs the risk of having a negative reputation follow him in subsequent years.

Case 5.3: Inappropriate Language

- Prejudiced language can be offensive—*should* be offensive—to everybody, not just people whose identities are targeted by the language. This is why even though, as far as she knows, none of Ms. Lindquist's students identify as Chinese or Chinese American, she has an obligation to address the use of the term. It's important to remember, as well, that we send an implicit message to students who are the targets of all kinds of bias that they are unsafe when we choose not to address situations like this.
- On a related note, sometimes students who are offended by terms such as "Chinese fire drill," or "retard," or phrases such as "that's so gay" do not feel empowered to say so, especially when

they experience biases or inequities related to the identities targeted by such language. They know that, in many cases, there will be a social price to pay for speaking up. So we never should assume people are not offended simply because nobody says she or he is offended.

- The more energy we put into creating an equitable, welcoming classroom and school climate at the beginning of the year, the easier it is to sustain such a climate throughout the year. It is important to provide students (and ourselves) with the tools necessary to discuss difficult issues and to practice those skills early and often rather than trying to scramble to do so when something troubling happens.

Case 5.4: Multicultural Day Parade

- Ms. Morrison used the words "ethnic" and "cultural" inter-changeably when describing the type of clothing that would be showcased in the parade. Typically, *ethnicity* is used to describe a person's ancestral, geographical background while *culture* is used to describe the norms of a group that could include people from various ethnicities. Additionally, *nationality* refers to the country of citizenship (which is not something that everybody has in an official sense) while *race* generally refers to groups of people identified by skin color and other attributes. It is important to note that each of these concepts is, to one extent or another, *socially constructed*—that is, they are classification systems designed by humans rather than scientifically based. (This is why a Colombian citizen can be considered white in Colombia but Latino in the United States.)
- Many schools incorporate a Diversity or Multicultural Day within their school year instead of integrating diversity in deeper, more thoughtful ways or instead of addressing inequities that may exist. Sometimes, in these sorts of events, students who feel alienated because of the way in which they are treated based on their identities throughout the year are asked to showcase their differences from the cultural "norm," which could further alienate them from their peers. It is important to consider how these

deeper issues of alienation and inequity could be addressed by the Diversity Committee.

- Ms. Morrison described the special clothing as "costumes," which is a word many people associate with Halloween or make-believe play clothes. As a result, this use of the word to describe clothing that youth associate with their cultural heritages could trivialize their cultures.

- Ms. Morrison had clear expectations of what she considered to be parade-worthy clothing. She assumed that students would be able to understand the notion of ethnic heritage and act accordingly. Once she realized otherwise, as with Keisha and Emily, she asserted her judgment and failed to see how their definition of "cultural clothing" was different from hers. Notice that Keisha was dismissed without consideration of the possibility that she, as an African American, might not have been able to trace her heritage to somewhere outside the United States or have access to clothing that she identifies as representing her ethnic background. Similarly, Emily may not know her ethnic background or have resources to acquire clothing for the event. Ms. Morrison failed to capture the opportunity to learn more about how her students self-identify.

Case 5.5: A Place to Study

- A quiet and isolated space might not be available in all students' homes. Moreover, not all students will value quiet isolation over the ability to work on homework collectively, as a family. If a collective approach is valued, then the pencil case probably would also be considered community property. Ms. Grady might have been setting up Shua to create conflict in his family by expecting him to tell his siblings that they were not allowed to use his materials. Furthermore, the collective use (and possible misplacement) of writing utensils does not necessarily reflect a need for additional donations or resources.

- Note that the scenario does not indicate whether Shua's homework situation negatively affected his academic success. This lack of indication raises questions about the appropriateness of discussing it at a conference, when doing so might create distance between the family and teacher. Additionally, Ms. Grady assumed that Shua's parents would not follow through on recommendations for providing additional learning support at home. This kind of assumption could have a negative impact upon Shua's learning, despite the fact that Ms. Grady had good intentions.

- Ms. Grady is worried about whether or not Shua is completing homework by himself. Would she have this same worry for a student who turned in homework without food stains or items crossed out instead of erased? Is it possible that Shua's brother is helping him, *perhaps even teaching him*, which is a good outcome? Consider how this sort of "help" might be interpreted differently based on the cultural norms of the student who is being helped and of his family.

Case 6.1: Task Force

- This case provides an opportunity to explore the kinds of barriers that might inhibit some parents and guardians from participating in afternoon or evening activities at schools, such as financial constraints that limit access to childcare or transportation, as well as work schedules for people who work multiple jobs. Language barriers could also limit participation if translators are not available. It is important to note that due to these and other barriers, a lack of parent involvement should not be assumed to be a lack of concern.
- When planning to solicit parent input and improve attendance at decision-making meetings, it is important to consider the school's *history* of outreach. Have under-represented families felt welcome or irrelevant? Might they be indifferent because they feel that their voices are not heard in the school?
- A posting on a district Web site is not an effective mechanism for announcing a meeting if the goal is to attract a diversity of parents and guardians. A newsletter might also not be an effective forum for announcing a task force meeting, depending on the home languages of students and their families.

Case 6.2: Teaching Race with *Huckleberry Finn*

- It might be easy to assume because Samuel was the only student in Ms. Kohl's class who responded publicly to the language in *Huck Finn* that he was the only student offended by it. We should remember, though, that students choose not to speak up for a variety of reasons. Some may remain silent in the face of bias because they know there is a social price to pay for speaking up or because they do not feel they will be heard by their teachers.

- Although Samuel's conduct and language was disruptive to the lesson, it is important to consider the circumstances which led to his outburst. Samuel displayed signs of becoming uncomfortable with what he might have perceived as a hostile environment, but Ms. Kohl allowed for the activity to continue. Punishing Samuel for his actions could send the message that he was not allowed to feel how he did and that Ms. Kohl's actions were acceptable because she was in a position of authority.

- Words are powerful—especially words such as the n-word with long, oppressive histories. It is a luxury of white privilege to see that word in a novel or poem or short story and to think of it solely as a marker of a certain historical time and place. Unfortunately, people who have been targeted with the word do not have that luxury, so we should consider carefully how, if at all, we want to introduce the n-word or similarly derogatory terms into our classroom communities. Certainly, if we choose to do so, it is a mistake to do so with no prior conversation or agreement regarding how to handle it in ways that do not alienate students.

- Too often when students learn about race and racism in school, they learn about them solely in the past tense, maybe through novels such as *Huckleberry Finn* or *To Kill a Mockingbird*. It is important to try to remember that race and racism remain relevant today and to help students make that connection so that we avoid contributing to the perception that racism was solved with the Civil Rights movement and the presidential election of Barack Obama.

Case 6.3: Diverse Friends Day

- It is important to acknowledge that Mr. Carbondale has good intentions; that he sees himself as an advocate for his students and that he demonstrates enthusiasm about the growing diversity in his school. It is equally important, though, to distinguish between appreciating diversity and advocating for equity. Events such as Diverse Friends Day are about the former, about racial *harmony*, but they are not necessarily about racial *equity*. They do not address underlying racial tensions or inequities, which is why some of the students of color might be opposed to them. It is important to examine the amount of time and resources that are allocated to celebrating diversity as compared with the time and resources devoted to building an equitable learning environment.

- This case provides an important opportunity to discuss the ways in which disenfranchised students, including students of color, are often put in positions to have to do the diversity educating. In this case, students of color are being asked to make themselves more vulnerable than some of them already feel at West River High School. When we use activities such as Diverse Friends Day, we sometimes are assuming that students enter into the experience equally, on a level playing field. Usually this is a bad assumption, which is part of what Pam, Tariq, and Julio are explaining to Mr. Carbondale.

- Although he had good intentions and, perhaps, because of the effects of his own racial privilege, Mr. Carbondale could not have known the full community's attitudes about this type of an event unless he solicited opinions from a diverse group of people, not just his principal. People who are involved with this type of decision-making always should elicit feedback from a diversity of people—including people who will be most greatly affected by the decision—before proceeding.

- Many—perhaps *most*—"diversity" initiatives in schools might encourage some level of cultural sharing, but fall short of creating a more equitable learning environment for disenfranchised students. These initiatives, when not carried out in conjunction with attention to racial or other inequities, can contribute to the very conditions they are being designed, ostensibly, to counteract.

Case 6.4: Terms of Endearment

- Even if—and this is a very big *if*—Reggie sincerely wasn't offended by Anthony's use of the term, it was very likely that other students, such as Keisha, *were* offended, including students who were not African American.
- Reggie's discomfort as Ms. Lawson prodded him about the situation might suggest that, in some ways, he really *wasn't* fine with Anthony using the n-word around him. In some social contexts, people who are the targets of oppressive language, whether the users of that language are intending to be offensive or not, might feel at least a temporary need to play along and pretend they are not offended, knowing there is a social price to pay for speaking up.
- There might also be cases in which students, hearing words such as the n-word used as a matter of course in popular culture, are not completely tuned into the words' histories or even their full contemporary implications. This is why it is important for us, as educators, to inform ourselves about words and phrases used by our students that are discriminatory, from variations on the n-word to "retard" or "that's so gay."
- Ms. Lawson felt prepared to take instructional advantage of the diversity in her school but she was not prepared to facilitate difficult conversations, such as one about the use of the n-word, with her students. As educators, we must equip ourselves with strategies for engaging students in conversations about these issues: not doing so could suggest that we condone bias or injustice.

Case 6.5: An Uncomfortable Field Trip

- It can be easy when we observe students behaving in ways that we interpret as inappropriate to find fault with them without wondering whether we have created the conditions for their behavior. By joking and laughing, Kevin and Alejandro might have been masking their discomfort or finding a small measure of comfort with each other in an uncomfortable setting. Back in the classroom, their peers also made light of the field trip. Perhaps there was something about their experience at the agency, including noticing the lack of diversity there, that made them question the notion that, with hard work and good grades, they too could work there. It's important to try to have the humility to consider how students might experience a learning activity differently from how we might experience it.

- Although Ms. Anderson felt that the experience was a failure, and blamed this failure at least in part on the fact that she tried to do it with "the wrong students," the day might have gone better with some fairly simple adjustments. For example, Ms. Anderson could have prepared her students for the symbols of wealth and lack of diversity they might encounter at the agency.

- A major social stressor on low-income students has to do with their families being unable to afford name-brand clothes and the newest fashions. Even in schools with school uniform policies, shoes often become a marker of status. As teachers, it's important that we avoid increasing this stressor, especially by connecting it to a school activity.

Case 7.1: Boys versus Girls Trivia Contest

- It's always a good idea to use a variety of teaching strategies to engage students and to involve them in classroom decision-making. However, we also have an obligation to ensure that the learning environment is free of bias and stereotypes. In this particular case, Mr. Williams showed subtle and not so subtle bias. For example, he referred to his class as "guys," which was subtle, and threatened to seat students based on gender, assuming that doing so would make the class unhappy, which was not so subtle. His good intentions did not make his actions any less biased. This is why it is so important to reflect on the biases we are carrying into the classroom with us and how these biases are communicated to students.

- Mr. Williams allowed students to make disparaging remarks and addressed them only as a disruption to the game rather than as gender bias. In doing so he missed an opportunity to help his students understand that sexism has harmful personal and social consequences. Also, perhaps unintentionally, he condoned the behavior by not addressing it.
- Research has shown for years that gender is not a simple "girl" and "boy" binary. Young people today are increasingly embracing identities that do not fit so easily into simplistic boxes. Some youth might be unsure about their gender identities. Identifying as transgender or as gender non-conforming in any other way is not so socially accepted that we can assume youth will be open about it. This is one reason why allowing the joking, even if you think it is good natured, can be harmful. It puts young people who do not fit into these simple categories in a position to feel socially like they have to play along with the jokes even if they feel repressed by them.

Case 7.2: Gender Bias with a Smile

- During the past ten years or so, brain research has become an increasingly popular part of conversations about education and learning. It's important, though, to recognize the difference between brain research and stereotyping, the latter of which is what Mr. Cameron did in this case.
- Mr. Cameron was pleasant and well intentioned. However, his comments were uninformed and biased, so they had the potential to do damage whether or not he intended them to do so. Unfortunately, inequity is frequently perpetuated by affable people who would be horrified to know how their words or actions are affecting the people around them.
- It might be easy to assume that Ms. Braxton's lesson about women scientists was relevant only to the young women in her class. However, this case presents an opportunity to discuss how important it is for young men to learn about sexism and gender bias and for all students to have access to an inclusive curriculum. Just as this kind of a lesson might help young women to realize

they can have a future in science, it might encourage young men to avoid perpetuating gender biases. Both of these functions are equally important.

Case 7.3: Timmy's Gender Nonconformity

- It can be easy for those of us who have not felt the sting of prejudice to feel that young children are not ready to have conversations about issues such as gender identity or race or class. However, if individual prejudice and group bias is present, it's our best evidence that youth, however young they might be, are already thinking about and trying to process these issues. If Ms. Grover fails to address this issue directly with her students, she cheats all of them out of an opportunity to develop a deeper understanding of their own and others' identities. Another risk of not intervening in a more direct way is that the failure to do so implicitly could send the message to Timmy and other students who are not gender conforming—who do not identify with stereotypical gender labels—that they are not safe or welcome in Ms. Grover's classroom.

- Some students in this case were taking on the role of "gender police," policing each other into gender conformity through peer pressure. A failure to notice and address these early forms of policing could result in the internalization of the pressure to conform, as well as heightened policing by the students.

- Timmy's teachers tended to see students' treatment of him as teasing or bullying. It's important to remember that teasing and bullying are often rooted in other issues related to institutional culture. Those underlying issues cannot be addressed only by interrupting the teasing or bullying, which are symptoms of the institutional culture. In order to address the issues in this case in the longer term, Ms. Grover will need to ask herself what it is about her classroom culture, or the school culture, or the broader societal culture that encourages or even rewards the type of teasing and bullying that Timmy was experiencing.

Case 7.4: Internet Objectification

- Students who are being bullied or harassed are frequently reluctant to report it for fear that the social cost of doing so will exceed the pain associated with the bullying or harassment. Similarly, students might be reluctant to stand up for others who are being discriminated against, bullied, or harassed because they worry about the social cost of doing so. This is why it is so important for schools to have robust and comprehensive anti-discrimination, anti-bullying, and anti-bias policies and programs that are active rather than reactive.
- On a similar note, youth who are being judged negatively on their appearances might worry about seeming weak minded if they speak up. They might worry that this could result in them being targeted in an intensified way. This, again, is why it is important for us to learn how to recognize the symptoms of bullying, harassment, and discrimination, and then to address the issues underlying them rather than only responding to individual incidents.
- It can be easy to imagine a situation like this as a simple matter of Tyler being childish and inappropriate. However, there are deeper issues here that need to be uncovered and addressed if the goal is to create and sustain an equitable and just learning environment. For example, heterosexual young men often participate in this sort of thing in order to assert their heterosexual masculinity. It also can be understood as a sense of entitlement to and need for control, which is at the root of much sexual harassment. Unfortunately, when schools attempt in any way to address issues such as online harassment, they often treat symptoms like inappropriate behavior without considering these underlying dynamics.

Case 8.1: A "Surprise" Fire Drill

- A high-pitched, intermittent blast along with the chaos that may ensue from a fire drill can be traumatic for some students who are on the Autism spectrum. For some people, the effects can last for days, or even weeks, and compromise their ability to function in the classroom. It's important to note that a student's ability to do well in a mainstream classroom is not an indicator of how severely they might react to particular stimuli or events, and this reaction itself might cause confusion with the other students. There are many strategies to avoid this sort of trauma, including, in this case, noise-reducing headphones.

- Ms. Foster was concerned about creating an environment in which all of her students, including Aiden, were given an equal opportunity to respond to the surprise fire drill. While her intentions were good, the impact of her desire to remove him from the classroom or deny him the headphones could be harmful. This case provides an interesting opportunity to consider the relationship between practicing *equality*, wherein all students are treated the same, and practicing *equity*, wherein all students are provided the supports they need in order to give them an equal opportunity to succeed.

Case 8.2: Insufficient Accommodations

- This case points, among other things, to the tension between *equality* and *equity*. All students are invited on the same field trip, which would constitute a sort of equality. But once on the field trip not all students have the same access to learning opportunities, which is an obvious inequity. The best "accommodations" should provide equitable experiences rather than equal experiences. Consider how this tension manifests in other educational scenarios.
- Making choices for equity can be a difficult task. There often is a lot to consider, including what Sonia Nieto has called the "sociopolitical context of schooling." It might be tempting to look at this one event and think, "It's just one field trip so it's no big deal if Justin is separated from the class so everybody else can experience the hike." But if we step back and consider the situation more broadly, we begin to see that students like Justin often experience little slights, little fragments of inequity that taken together could constitute a fairly exclusionary school experience.

This is why it is important to consider these single events in their larger contexts.

- Ms. Thurston might feel compelled to address this issue with Justin and Ms. Parsons exclusively, but it is important to realize that it should be addressed with all of her students. By engaging them in a process of community-building and problem-solving, she would demonstrate that Justin is an integral part of the class community. Perhaps a future unit could encourage students to look at other ways in which inequity concerns come into play, perhaps by evaluating issues in their own communities.

- Although Ms. Thurston was mindful enough to call the park and inquire about accommodations, she took for granted that Justin would have a learning experience that roughly paralleled that of his classmates when Ms. Parsons told her that accommodations were available. This reflects a sort of privilege that both Ms. Thurston and Ms. Parsons (as well as other people without mobility challenges) experience, but may not understand. Had Ms. Thurston asked for clarification about the available accommodations, she would not have been surprised upon arriving at the park. More importantly, she would have had more of an opportunity to make alternate, more equitable plans for her students.

Case 8.3: Nut Allergy

- As the number of students being diagnosed with food allergies increases, educators need to create policies that ensure student safety. For some students who, like Katelyn, have a nut or legumes allergy diagnosis, even minimal exposure to peanuts or other nuts can mean a trip to the hospital or even death. Katelyn's mother advocated for her safety because she understood the extreme consequences that could occur if Katelyn was accidentally exposed to nuts. To her, that was more important than another parent's or guardian's desire to share an experience with their child. For adults who do not understand the potential severity of allergies, Ms. Thomas's request could have felt like an imposition. Mr. Hughes had taken many steps to protect Katelyn in the classroom, but he might have benefited, as well, by helping to educate other students' parents and guardians about the seriousness of Katelyn's allergies.

- When he attempted to address the growing tension in the classroom, Mr. Hughes noticed that the conversation was causing Katelyn additional grief. He also noticed that some of the students' comments were reflecting what was being communicated to them at home. Rather than causing additional tension by directly confronting what some of his students' parents and guardians were saying at home, Mr. Hughes could refocus the conversation on the classroom community and what equity and inclusion looks like in that context. Whatever he chooses to do, it is important to take the spotlight off Katelyn and her mother.

- Although he might have wanted to validate the frustration felt by the parents and guardians who hoped to join the field trip but for whom there was no space, it was equally important that Mr. Hughes defend his commitment to advocating for Katelyn. In this sense, this case provides an opportunity to discuss the importance of staying committed to ideals of equity and social justice in the classroom, even in the face of complaints that might come, as a result, from parents and guardians.

Case 9.1: A New Club

- Gay–Straight Alliances and other student organizations built around particular affinity groups are designed to provide points of connection and systems of support for students who are marginalized in the larger school culture. This is why asking Lorraine, Jeff, Terrence, and Hu to start a Diversity Club instead defeats the purpose of the GSA. The fact that the students are taking the lead on creating that space of safety for themselves can also indicate that the school is not doing enough to create a safe atmosphere for them.

- In this sense, Ms. Livingsworth's solution is yet another indication of the school's lack of a sense of urgency to ensure an equitable learning environment for LGBQ students (not to mention staff, faculty, and parents and guardians). By trying, in theory, to be "inclusive," the principal risks further alienating students who already might be feeling alienated.

- Ms. Livingsworth's primary concern appears to be the possibility of alienating families she imagines to be in the majority: conservative Christian families who, she worries, will be offended by a GSA. She might be right that some of those families would respond negatively to a GSA in their children's schools. On the other hand, some of those families might include LGBQ people. Certainly, if she allowed the students to start the GSA, Ms. Livingsworth and her administrative team, along with the teachers, would have work to do explaining it, and even defending it, to some families. However, choosing diversity and equity policy and practice based on these sorts of concerns all but guarantees the persistence of inequity.

Case 9.2: Date Auction

- Although Mr. Hanson has good intentions in wanting students to take ownership of the project, his silence implicitly condones the students' idea and the comments made by a couple of them. We must remember that the laughter among the other students in response to Nate's comments does not necessarily reflect their *agreement.* This case offers an important opportunity to discuss how peer pressure can encourage complicity with bias, even among people who comprise the groups being targeted by the bias.

- It might be easy to assume that because none of the students' sexual orientations were named explicitly in the case, or because none of the students explicitly claimed a lesbian, gay, bisexual, or queer identity (LGBQ), everybody at the council meeting identified as heterosexual. It is important to point out that this could be a faulty assumption. It also provides an important opportunity to discuss the danger of those sorts of assumptions.

- Many homeless youth struggle to find acceptance, either because they are homeless or because of some dimension of their identities. In fact, LGBQ youth who are homeless sometimes identify rejection due to their sexual and/or gender identities as one reason for their homelessness. Additionally, homeless youth are often sexually exploited. A date auction, and other sorts of heteronormative popularity contests, can also perpetuate feelings of inadequacy among some students and reinforce the destructive notion that some people are more worthy of adulation than others. It is important to consider how all of these conditions conflict with the council's well-intentioned desire to educate their peers about youth homelessness.

- This scenario presents opportunities for many forms of bias, including racism (and white privilege) and classism, in addition to sexism (and male privilege) and heterosexism (and heteronormativity). For example, although the school community is relatively affluent, this type of event is accessible only to students who can afford to participate; the event can easily turn into a display of who has more access to wealth. Additionally, bidding on someone's worth could be experienced by some members of the school community as a reminder of historical atrocities such as the slave trade. Try to consider what other well-intentioned types of fundraisers commonly held at schools advantage wealthier students and families.

Case 9.3: Outed at School

- This case provides an important opportunity to discuss the concept of heteronormativity—the way in which heterosexuality is normalized in subtle and not so subtle ways in schools. Examples might include the ways in which dances and other events are marketed, assumptions that all students have "mothers and fathers," conversations about dating, and discussions about literature and history in which people are presumed to be heterosexual even when no particular sexual orientation is specified.

- One of the reasons Mr. Brooks was cautious about how to proceed was that there might be a student in his class who identified as LGBQ or who had a relative who did. This possibility, or *probability*, is why it is so important never to allow homophobic language to go unnamed. Doing so can make all students feel the way Mr. Brooks felt when he was a student: that teachers condone it.

- A common concern about introducing conversations about sexual orientation, homophobia, or heterosexism (discrimination against LGBQ people) in schools is that youth of certain ages are not old enough to talk about such matters. However, youth who are using homophobic or heterosexist language *are* already talking about sexual orientation, and are doing so in ways that are hurtful to their LGBQ peers or peers who have LGBQ friends or family members. Children of any age can talk about these issues when provided with effective facilitation.

Case 9.4: Two Moms

- Often, when somebody thinks kids of a certain age are not old enough to talk about an issue, whether related to race or sexual orientation or any other identity, they are thinking primarily of kids from *privileged* identities. In this case, Denise is already beginning to experience bias from her peers and it is likely that she has witnessed her mothers experiencing bias, as well. As a general rule, we might say that if students are old enough to express or experience bias or injustice, they are old enough to talk about that bias or injustice. These conversations can occur as early as preschool.
- It might not always be possible to completely avoid conflict and controversy if we are fully committed to creating and sustaining a bias-free, equitable, and just classroom environment. This is because doing so requires us to respond to the kinds of situations to which Ms. Ribiero was responding in this case. One measure of a school's commitment to ensuring an equitable learning environment is its persistence to that commitment even in the face of controversy.

Case 10.1: Student Translator

- Although Marcella agreed to be an interpreter for the conversation between her mother and Mr. Clark, teachers always should ask parents' or guardians' permission before requesting this sort of a favor from one of their children. Mr. Clark had no way of knowing the cultural dynamics at play in his request.

- Mr. Clark intended to empower Marcella by praising her for her abilities. The impact of his words, however, might not have been so positive. His praise for her ability to speak two languages might have made her mother feel ashamed or embarrassed since she was not yet proficient in English.

- Rather than using a student to discuss a student issue with a parent, Mr. Clark might have used a bilingual staff member as an interpreter or have had Maria explain to her mother that Mr. Clark would be calling her to arrange a time to meet with him and a translator.

Case 10.2: English Only

- Research has shown for decades that English-only policies are harmful to the morale *and the learning* of students who are learning English. These policies also contribute to the alienation of their parents and families. Given these realities, it is important to consider that these policies are often ideological responses, reactive in nature and not based on evidence of best teaching practices.

- Ms. Mancini and Ms. de Leon are in a difficult situation. There are times in all teachers' careers when we must make decisions about the extent to which we will implement policies and practices that we believe are harmful to students or even to colleagues. Ms. Mancini and Ms. de Leon will need to be extremely mindful of the implications of their decisions about how to proceed.

- Students who are learning English in school can feel exhausted by the end of the day because of how hard they are concentrating on language while also focusing on other aspects of school. Being able to speak in their home languages for brief periods throughout the day provides some relief so they are better able to focus. This reality might be difficult to understand for people who have not experienced being submersed in an environment in which a language other than their home language is spoken. One way to cultivate this sort of empathy is having teachers sit through a sample lesson or staff development that is conducted entirely in a language with which they are not familiar, then to follow the experience with a conversation about how it felt. Although these experiences do not recreate the full magnitude of discomfort that students who are learning English might experience in an English-only environment, they offer a short, and sometimes powerful, glimpse into that experience.

- Despite popular perception, contemporary immigrants who arrive in the United States not speaking English are learning English more quickly than any previous generation of immigrants. It is important to challenge the stereotype that immigrants do not want to learn English or do not want their children to learn English. It is also important to remind ourselves that many people whose families have been in the United States for multiple generations have ancestors who were discriminated against due to *their* inability to speak English.

Case 10.3: Family Night

- The teachers designed the event based on their perceptions of what would make an ideal family night. They assumed that all parents would arrive exactly at the event start time, sit quietly, listen, and then go home. One thing they did not consider was the importance in many cultures of social interaction, communication, and connection. The importance placed upon these dynamics does not reflect disinterest in school or in an event's official program.
- The teachers were very thoughtful in translating the flier for Family Night. However, they did not think to provide translation for the evening's program or the handout. It could be the case, given this fact, that the ELL families were discussing the presentation and helping to translate it for each other, standing in the back in order to avoid disrupting other attendees.
- Families might not have seemed interested in the online resources handout because it was not translated or because of a lack of access to a computer with internet access at home. Alternatively,

they might not have asked questions if the handout was self-explanatory or if they felt it would be a burden to the teachers to stay and answer questions after the event had ended.

- The event produced a high turnout from families who do not typically attend functions at Crestwood. This is an accomplishment that cannot be quantified. Instead of feeling discouraged, Mr. Nelson and the other teachers might focus on finding ways to build on this accomplishment.

Case 11.1: An Assigned Nickname

- Given the power dynamics between teachers and students, sometimes a choice really isn't a choice. Sarai might have agreed to the name change out of respect for Ms. Goodwin or out of a desire to avoid the uncomfortable situation of having to "correct" Ms. Goodwin's pronunciation of her name. In either case, it's important to be sensitive to the situations in which we place students, even unintentionally. Ms. Goodwin also commented that the name Sara is a pretty name, so Sarai might not express a desire to go by her given name if she wants to please her teacher.
- Some parents and guardians feel, for a variety of reasons, that they are not in a position to challenge their children's teachers. Sarai's mother nodded in agreement with Sarai's nickname but might not be comfortable with the decision, which could explain her change in behavior during the conference.
- Names are important. In many cases they tie us to our ancestors or to the places from where our ancestors hailed, and these ties can be particularly strong for immigrants or first-generation U.S. citizens. Changes to a child's name during their school years can remain with them throughout her or his lifetime.

Case 11.2: I'm not Black

- Rather than assigning Abiola a mentor based on her own criteria for who would be best, Ms. Lee could have asked for a volunteer. She also could have asked Abiola whether he wanted a mentor. Certainly, though, she should have been more careful not to turn her mentor program into a social experiment by presuming she could help create a bridge between the African American and Nigerian students by matching Warren with Abiola.

- The trouble with color blindness is that it masks not just difference but the ramifications of difference. When we are determined not to see difference it can become all too easy to disregard inequities or biases that are associated with difference. Students' racial and ethnic (and other) identities influence the ways in which they experience school, largely because people's assumptions and expectations of them are informed by those racial and ethnic (and other) identities. As long as racial bigotry and injustice exist, color blindness merely masks this reality, blocking us from seeing and addressing its roots.

- In many, if not *most*, cases in which new waves of immigrants have entered the United States, those immigrants have experienced tremendous amounts of bias and injustice. This is even true, for example, for waves of Irish and Italian immigrants, who experienced bigotry similar to what Mexican and Central American immigrants experience today. This case provides an important opportunity to reflect on why this pattern persists. Consider what makes people whose own ancestors immigrated to the U.S., perhaps facing bigotry in the process, turn around and aim their bigotry at today's immigrants.

Case 11.3: A Legacy of Privilege on the Soccer Field

- This case provides an important opportunity to discuss the ways in which national policy concerns are often, and unfortunately, debated on the backs of youth. This is especially true of immigration and language policies.

- Sometimes when people support their positions on issues by referring to a "legacy" or "tradition," they are subtly demonstrating a sense of entitlement or a fear of change. Many educational inequities and biases remain in schools in the name of "tradition," such as through the continued use of stereotype-inspired American Indian athletic team mascots.

Case 11.4: Parent Involvement

- Although Mr. Rolnick provided various opportunities for parents to volunteer, many could be interpreted as simple tasks meant to assist teachers rather than as meaningful ways to engage students. Although some parents or guardians might enjoy filing books or making copies, others might prefer being involved more directly by tutoring, reading aloud, or assisting with other learning activities in the classroom or with their own children at home.

- Mr. Rolnick equated volunteering with parent involvement, but these are very different in nature. Parent involvement can take many forms, including simply asking children about their school day, encouraging them to read or do their homework, or following up on a phone call from the teacher. Joel's parents were involved, as they attended conferences, returned forms, and offered to address concerns at home. It is important that we do not mistake their hesitance to volunteer at the school as a lack of concern for their children's learning.

- One barrier to family involvement that receives too little attention is some parents' and guardians' own negative experiences with school. An experience some people take for granted, such as walking into an elementary school for a meeting and feeling welcome and appreciated, might not be a universal experience. For people who felt alienated at school, walking into the building can feel like entering a new cultural space. It can be uncomfortable, perhaps even intimidating. Some parents and guardians might still see in schools the inequities and biases they experienced as students and thus might choose to involve themselves in their children's education without coming to the school. This reality can be particularly difficult to see for those of us who always have felt validated at school.

Case 11.5: My Uncle

- In some cultures all elders, or at least close family friends who are elders, are referred to as "Uncle" or "Aunt" as a sign of respect. Abdi's uncle might have been unrelated to him by blood, but still a trusted friend who went to the school in place of his father. Because Ms. Klein and Ms. Larson's cultural views only recognized those terms as referring to family members, they assumed that Abdi's family, and others in the school who acted in a similar manner, were being deceitful. This kind of assumption can have a deleterious impact upon relationships between teachers and students, as well as students' families.

- Ms. Klein made an assumption about whether her concerns would be communicated to the father, and she felt frustrated as she believed that Abdi's behavior would not change because his father did not attend the conference. Unfortunately, she discredited Abdi's mother's authority based only on her observations from Meet the Teacher night. A more constructive, and perhaps more effective, way for her to view the situation would have been to realize that Abdi's mother was *very much* engaged in addressing his behavior concerns. This was evident because she addressed his behavior at Meet the Teacher night and also attended the conference with an additional influential person in Abdi's life.

- Students whose home lives are blends of multiple cultures can feel conflicted between the norms of those cultures. A student who feels embarrassed because of some aspect of her identity, especially when teachers respond negatively to it, might respond by disengaging from school. Alternatively, the student's desire to be accepted by the school community might cause a change in behavior that can be at odds with traditions in the house, causing conflict within the family.

References

Brown, K. D. and Kraehe, A. M. (2010) "The complexities of teaching the complex: Examining how future educators construct understandings of sociocultural knowledge and schooling," *Educational Studies*, 46, 91–115.

Darling-Hammond, L. (2006) *Powerful Teacher Education: Lessons from Exemplary Programs*. San Francisco, CA: Jossey-Bass.

Foster, R. H., McBeth, M. K., and Clemons, R. S. (2010) "Public policy pedagogy: Mixing methodologies using case studies," *Journal of Public Affairs Education*, 16(4), 517–540.

Gallucci, K. (2006) "Learning concepts with cases," *Journal of College Science Teaching*, 36(2), 16–20.

Gorski, P. C. (in press) "Imagining equity literacy," *Teaching Tolerance*.

Heitzmann, R. (2008) "Case study instruction in teacher education: Opportunity to develop students' critical thinking, school smarts and decision making," *Education*, 128(4), 523–542.

Jones, K. (2005) "Widening the lens: The efficacy of the case method in helping direct practice MSW students understand and apply mezzo and macro dimensions of practice," *Social Work Education*, 24(2), 197–211.

Leonard, E. C. and Cook, R. A. (2010) "Teaching with cases," *Journal of Teaching in Travel & Tourism*, 10, 95–101.

Naumes, W. and Naumes, M. (1999) *The Art and Craft of Case Writing*. Thousand Oaks, CA: Sage.

Nieto, S., and Bode, P. (2011) *Affirming Diversity: The Sociopolitical Context of Multicultural Education*. Boston, MA: Pearson.

Noblitt, L., Vance, D. E. and Smith, M. L. D. (2010) "A comparison of case study and traditional teaching methods for improvement of oral communication and critical-thinking skills," *Journal of College Science Teaching*, 39(5), 26–32.

REFERENCES

Swalwell, K. (2011) "Why our students need 'equity literacy'," *Teaching Tolerance Blog*, http://www.tolerance.org/blog/why-our-students-need-equity-literacy, accessed January 13, 2013.

Tarnvik, A. (2007) "Revival of the case method: A way to retain student-centered learning in a post-PBL era," *Medical Teacher*, 29, 32–36.

Walker, C. (2009) "Teaching policy theory and its application to practice using long structured case studies: An approach that deeply engages under-graduate students," *International Journal of Teaching and Learning in Higher Education*, 20(2), 214–225.

Yadav, A. and Barry, B. E. (2009) "Using case-based instruction to increase ethical understanding in engineering: What do we know? What do we need?," *International Journal of Engineering Education*, 25(1), 138–143.

Yadav, A., Shaver, G. M. and Meckl, P. (2010) "Lessons learned: Implementing the case teaching method in a mechanical engineering course," *Journal of Engineering Education*, 99(1), 55–69.